MW00334555

the ALTUCHER CONFIDENTIAL

IDEAS FOR A WORLD OUT OF BALANCE

Writers of the Round Table Press

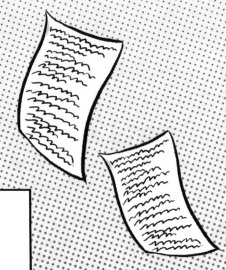

THE ALTUCHER CONFIDENTIAL

© 2011 JAMES ALTUCHER

ROUND TABLE COMICS
@rndtablecomics
www.roundtablecomics.com

Based on the blog by JAMES ALTUCHER
www.jamesaltucher.com

ROUND TABLE COMPANIES
1670 VALENCIA WAY
MUNDELEIN, IL 60060, USA
PHONE: 815-346-2398

Executive editor: COREY MICHAEL BLAKE
Digital distribution: DAVID C. COHEN
Front cover illustration: NATHAN LUETH
Front cover layout design: NATHAN BROWN
Interior design/layout, back cover: SUNNY DiMARTINO
Proofreading: RITA HESS
Last looks: MARY LAINE

Printed in the United States of America

First edition: DEC 2011
10 9 8 7 6 5 4 3 2 1

LIBRARY OF CONGRESS CATALOGING-IN-PUBLICATION DATA
Altucher, James
The Altucher Confidential / James Altucher.—1st ed. p. cm.
ISBN: 978-1-939418-07-4
1. Humor. 2. Success in business. I. Title.

No part of this publication may be reproduced or transmitted in any form or by any means, mechanical or electronic, including photocopying and recording, or by any information storage and retrieval system, without permission in writing from author or publisher (except by a reviewer, who may quote brief passages and/or show brief video clips in a review).

the ALTUCHER CONFIDENTIAL

IDEAS FOR A WORLD OUT OF BALANCE

FROM THE MIND AND BLOG OF
JAMES ALTUCHER

ILLUSTRATED BY
NATHAN LUETH

SCRIPTED BY
NADJA BAER

TO CLAUDIA ...
SHE RE-DRAWS ME EVERY DAY.

PROSTITUTES, DRUGS, HBO AND THE BEST JOB EVER AT 3 IN THE MORNING

THE BEST JOB I EVER HAD WAS INTERVIEWING PROSTITUTES, JUNKIES, HOMELESS KIDS, AND OTHER RANDOM CREATURES AT THREE A.M.

THE JOB STARTED BECAUSE HBO DIDN'T HAVE A WEBSITE OR AN INTRANET. SO ONE WEEKEND I PUT THE HBO CAFETERIA MENU ON AN INTRANET I SET UP. THEN I PUT THEIR EMPLOYEE DATABASE ON THERE, THEN THEIR MOVIE DATABASE, AND SO ON. I FORGOT TO ASK FOR PERMISSION.

COMEDY CENTRAL CALLED ME AND ASKED ME IF I COULD HELP DO THE SAME THING FOR THEM.

MAYBE I HAD A SMALL CRUSH ON THE IT WOMAN THERE WHO ASKED ME. BUT I MIGHT'VE HAD A CRUSH ON EVERYONE BACK THEN.

YOU GUYS ARE GREAT AT DOING ORIGINAL TV SHOWS, HOW ABOUT LET ME DO AN ORIGINAL WEB SHOW?

I'LL ONLY DO IT IF YOU GIVE ME THE TIME SLOT FROM 3 TO 4 A.M. TO DO WHATEVER I WANT.

SORRY, WE SELL THAT TIME SLOT FOR INFOMERCIALS.

ELIZABETH L

HBO
Web Programming

SO THAT'S HOW I DID "III:AM" FOR 2.5 YEARS. EVERY TUESDAY NIGHT I WOULD GO OUT AT THREE A.M. AND INTERVIEW WHOEVER I COULD FIND.

IF YOU WERE OUT AND ABOUT AT 3 A.M. ON A TUESDAY NIGHT, THEN THERE'S A REASON. YOU PROBABLY DON'T WORK A REGULAR 9-5 JOB. YOU PROBABLY DON'T DO A REGULAR ANYTHING. YOU'RE OUT EITHER CAUSING TROUBLE OR AVOIDING IT.

1

I TURNED OVER EVERY ROCK IN THE CITY. FOR INSTANCE, THERE'S A BUS THAT GOES BACK AND FORTH FROM QUEENS TO RIKERS ISLAND. IT RUNS ALL NIGHT LONG BECAUSE IF SOMEONE CAN GET BAILED OUT, THEY GET OUT OF JAIL RIGHT THEN. THE BUS STOP HAD THE CONSTANT BUZZ OF MISFORTUNE.

ONCE SOMEONE GOT ON THAT BUS I NEVER SAW THEM AGAIN.

HOW MANY TIMES DID I FALL IN LOVE? I CAN'T EVEN BEGIN TO SAY. EVERYONE TRYING TO BELT OUT THEIR STORY AND BE HEARD IN THE MIDDLE OF THE NIGHT BECAUSE THE SHACKLES THAT SHUT THEM UP DURING THE DAY WERE SOUND ASLEEP.

FOR TWO YEARS I PUT FOUR INTERVIEWS A WEEK UP ON THE HBO WEBSITE WITH THE HELP OF A GREAT CREW OF PEOPLE AT HBO. EVERYONE HAD TO SIGN A RELEASE FORM AND PUT THEIR PHONE NUMBERS, WHICH FOR A WHILE WAS THE ONLY WAY I WOULD GET A DATE OR TWO WHEN SOMEONE CAUGHT MY EYE AND I'D CALL THEM THE DAY AFTER.

IT WAS A DIFFERENT WORLD. THE SAME LOCATIONS, BUT DIFFERENT RULES, DIFFERENT CUSTOMS, DIFFERENT CULTURES. THERE WAS THE WORKING WORLD, AND THEN THERE WERE THE FORGOTTEN OUTCASTS FROM THAT WORLD.

AND SO, HEATHER, WHAT WOULD YOU LIKE TO DO TO TONY?

I'D LIKE TO SLIT HIS NECK.

WHAT QUESTIONS DO YOU WANT TO ASK TONY?

IF HE'LL TAKE A KNIFE, CUT MY HEART OUT, AND EAT IT FOR DINNER.

THE SADDER AND MORE TWISTED A STORY WAS, THE MORE BEAUTIFUL TO ME.

ALL THE RULES WE THINK OF AS NORMAL SOCIETY ARE ALL MANUFACTURED. THERE'S NO SUCH THING AS NORMAL.

THERE'S A 3 A.M. RELIGION: THERE ARE TOO MANY SIDES OF LIFE TO COUNT. EACH WITH ITS OWN WAY OF ESCAPING THE CHAINS THAT BIND US TO THE DAY.

THE SADNESS WAS UNBEARABLE, BUT ONLY THEN DO YOU SEE GOD IN THEIR EYES LOOKING BACK.

HOW I SCREWED YASSER ARAFAT OUT OF $2MM (AND LOST $100MM IN THE PROCESS)

I NEEDED TO MAKE ONE HUNDRED MILLION DOLLARS PRETTY FAST. YOU KNOW HOW IT IS. THERE ARE BILLS TO PAY. THERE ARE THINGS YOU WANT TO DO IN LIFE. AT THE TIME (1999) I HAD RECENTLY MADE MONEY SELLING A COMPANY IN THE WEB SERVICES BUSINESS. AMONG OTHER THINGS, MY COMPANY MADE THE WEBSITE FOR THE MOVIE, "THE MATRIX." I KNEW I WAS NEO BUT I WOULDN'T BE ABLE TO TAKE THE RED PILL UNTIL I HAD MY FIRST HUNDRED MILLION.

THAT WAS THE PILL THAT WOULD LET ME BE A REAL PERSON. THE PILL THAT WOULD ALLOW ME TO BE FULLY ALIVE.

SO I CAME UP WITH AN IDEA. IT WAS A CATCHPHRASE AND I WOULD USE IT MANY TIMES OVER THE NEXT SIX MONTHS.

FIRST THERE WAS THE WIRELINE INTERNET.

THEN THERE WAS THE WIRELESS INTERNET.

WHICH WOULD BE TEN TIMES BIGGER.

THOSE THREE SENTENCES (OR MAYBE IT'S ONE IF YOU USE COMMAS) WERE MY PATH TO $100 MILLION. HERE'S WHAT YOU DO THEN ONCE YOU HAVE YOUR CATCHPHRASE. I HAD A BUSINESS PARTNER WHO WASN'T SHY. SO HE CALLED UP 20 COMPANIES IN THE WIRELESS SOFTWARE BUSINESS.

WE WANT TO BUY YOUR COMPANY.

WE HAD NO MONEY TO BUY ANYBODY BUT IF YOU EVER LET THAT SLOW YOU DOWN YOU MIGHT AS WELL RUN AROUND NAKED IN A FOOTBALL STADIUM WITH 60,000 PEOPLE WATCHING YOU.

ONE COMPANY RESPONDED. A COMPANY CALLED "MOBILELOGIC" OUT OF DENVER. THEY FLEW IN AND WE TOOK THEM OUT TO BREAKFAST AT THE ROYALTON HOTEL ON 44TH STREET. THE SORT OF PLACE RUPERT MURDOCH ORDERS THE PANCAKES, CHEWS IT UP, SPITS IT OUT WITHOUT SWALLOWING, AND THEN ORDERS GRANOLA TO BE HEALTHY.

IT'S FORTUNATE THAT YOU CALLED. ERICSSON JUST OFFERED US SEVENTEEN MILLION AND WE'RE THINKING OF TAKING IT.

WHY WOULD YOU TAKE THAT? WE'LL OFFER YOU $20 MILLION, HALF CASH, HALF STOCK. THAT STOCK ALONE WILL BE WORTH $100 MILLION OR MORE ONCE WE GO PUBLIC.

MOBILELOGIC CEO

WE HAVE FIVE OTHER COMPANIES WE'LL BUY AFTER YOU. YOU'LL BE PRESIDENT OF A MAJOR COMPANY THAT'S GOING PUBLIC, PRONTO. ERICSSON IS THE OLD GENERATION. BE A PART OF SOMETHING NEW AND EXCITING.

THEY TOOK OUR OFFER. WE QUICKLY WROTE UP A BINDING LOI, WHICH THEY SIGNED. NOW WE NEEDED TO PAY THEM $20 MILLION. WE KNEW WE COULD PAY HALF IN STOCK, SO THAT WAS EASY. THAT WAS A PIECE OF PAPER. NOW WE HAD TO COME UP WITH THE OTHER TEN.

SO, WITH SOME PARTNERS WHO WERE EXCELLENT MIDDLEMEN I STARTED GOING TO POTENTIAL INVESTORS. MARK PATTERSON, WHO WAS THEN VICE CHAIRMAN OF CSFB AND IS NOW THE HEAD OF MULTI-BILLION DOLLAR HEDGE FUND MAITLIN-PATTERSON, SET UP A CONFERENCE CALL WITH A FEW SMALL INVESTORS.

Henry Kravis: Head of private equity firm Kohlberg Kravis Roberts & Co.

Leo Hindery: Managing Partner of InterMedia private equity fund.

Jim McCann: CEO of 1-800-FLOWERS

Dennis Something-or-Other: Just sold Irish telecom company, worth a random billion.

NO PROBLEM. BECAUSE SUDDENLY I HAD A REAL ASSET. I HAD A BINDING LOI FOR A COMPANY WITH $5-10MM IN REVENUES (DESPITE MY PROPENSITY TO REMEMBER EVERY DETAIL OF MY CHILDHOOD, I CAN'T REMEMBER HOW MUCH IN REVENUES THIS COMPANY I WAS BUYING IN 1999 HAD).

I GAVE A FIFTEEN-MINUTE TALK. I DESCRIBED MY BACKGROUND AND THE COMPANY I HAD SOLD. THEN I USED MY CATCHPHRASE AND SCOPED OUT THE OPPORTUNITY AND THAT WAS THE CALL.

HENRY WANTS TO WIRE $5 MILLION RIGHT NOW.

THE ONLY PROBLEM: I WASN'T EVEN TOTALLY SURE WHAT MOBILELOGIC DID.

SO WHAT IS IT THAT YOUR COMPANY DOES?

UH, WELL, WE PROTECT DATA IN CORPORATE DATABASES BEING SENT OUT TO THE SALES FORCE THROUGH WIRELESS DEVICES THAT WE SET UP. THE DATA GOES TO THE SATELLITE AND THEN COMES DOWN TO OUR DEVICES.

DOESN'T DATA GO THROUGH CELLULAR TOWERS, NOT SATELLITES?

UH... YEAH... SOMETIMES.

BUT WE ONLY TOOK ONE FROM HIM. TOO MANY OTHER PEOPLE WANTED TO INVEST. EVERYONE ON THAT 15-MINUTE CONFERENCE CALL PUT IN ONE MILLION EACH.

AND THEY PUT $5 MILLION IN. FRANK QUATTRONE PUT MONEY IN. SAM WAKSAL, ALLEN & CO. CMGI. THE LIST GOES ON. WE WERE THE HOT INVESTMENT FOR THREE SECONDS.

SO WE CLOSED ON $30 MILLION DOLLARS AND BOUGHT OUR FIRST COMPANY. THEN WE BOUGHT A SECOND COMPANY. THEY HAD NOTHING TO DO WITH WIRELESS BUT THEY HAD PROFITS. WE'D BURY THEM IN THE IPO STORY BUT MAKE USE OF THEIR PROFITS. THEN WE BOUGHT A THIRD COMPANY. RIGHT AWAY WE WERE GETTING CALLS. AETHER SYSTEMS WANTED TO BUY US BUT WE SAID NO. THEY ONLY WANTED TO PAY $50 MILLION FOR THE COMPANY.

I COULD GET YOU $75 MILLION, NO PROBLEM.

BUT WE DIDN'T EVEN LISTEN TO HIM. IN THE ELEVATOR WE LAUGHED AT HIM. WHAT AN OLD FOOL! WE WERE GOING FOR AN IPO.

EVERY BANK CAME IN WITH A POWERPOINT AND A TEAM OF YOUNG PEOPLE TO PITCH US. GOLDMAN, CSFB, MERRILL, LEHMAN, ETC. CSFB WAS THE FRONT RUNNER BECAUSE FRANK QUATTRONE WAS AN INVESTOR BUT MERRILL MADE A STRONG PITCH. THE PITCH WAS FUNNY. THE TOP MERRILL BANKER WAS THERE. HE SAID TO THE ASSOCIATE ON THE DEAL, "JOHN, WALK THEM THROUGH THE NUMBERS." AND JOHN SAID, "UHH, MY NAME IS ROY." TWO OTHER THINGS I REMEMBER FROM THE PITCH: THE FIRST WAS, "HENRY BLODGET WILL BE THE ANALYST ON THIS DEAL. HE LOVES WIRELESS." WHICH MADE NO SENSE TO ME SINCE HE WAS AN INTERNET CONSUMER ANALYST.

Projected Net Worth: $900,000,000.00
*If market value is similar to Aether Systems

THE OTHER THING I REMEMBER WAS THE BACK PAGE OF THE PRESENTATION. THE BEAUTIFUL BACK PAGE. THE ONLY PAGE THAT MATTERED.

I DIDN'T KNOW HOW TO BE CEO OF THIS COMPANY. AND BECAUSE I DIDN'T REALLY KNOW ANY OF THE EMPLOY-EES OF THE COMPANIES WE WERE BUYING I WAS FEELING VERY SHY. I WOULD CALL MY SECRETARY BEFORE I ARRIVED AT WORK AND ASK HER IF ANYONE WAS IN THE HALLWAY AND COULD SHE PLEASE UNLOCK MY OFFICE DOOR. THEN I WOULD HURRY INTO THE OFFICE AND LOCK THE DOOR BEHIND ME.

EVENTUALLY THEY REPLACED ME AS CEO. EVEN LATER, WHEN WE HAD TO RAISE UP TO ANOTHER $70 MILLION, THEY ASKED ME TO STEP OFF AS A DIRECTOR ON THE BOARD. AT ONE POINT I ARRANGED FOR A REVERSE MERGER TO OCCUR. WE'D BE PUBLIC AT AT LEAST AT $100 MILLION VALUATION. BUT THE GUY BEHIND THE REVERSE MERGER TURNED OUT TO HAVE A CHECKERED PAST AND HAD SPENT SOME TIME IN JAIL IN 1969 FOR EITHER EMBEZZLEMENT OR SOMETHING TO DO WITH TRANSPORTING FAKE DIAMONDS.

JAMES ALT...
CEO
Director
Mergers & Acquisitions
Specialist in Lost Dollars
555
4...

BUT THAT'S ANOTHER STORY.

NONE OF THIS PORTRAYS ME IN A GOOD LIGHT AT ALL. EXCEPT FOR MAYBE THE FACT THAT I WAS A GOOD SALESMAN DURING THE GREATEST BUBBLE IN WORLD HISTORY. BUT IT WAS A DECADE AGO AND I DON'T MIND WHAT PEOPLE THINK.

BUT I DID LEARN SEVERAL THINGS THAT BECAME INCREDIBLY IMPORTANT TO ME LATER.

A) If you have to raise $30 million to start your business, it's probably not a good business.

B) Most M&A transactions don't work. Build your business. Don't buy it.

C) Traveling for business almost never generates more revenues. I've traveled repeatedly to the West Coast, Denver, England, Sweden, Germany, Georgia, Florida, Boston, etc. Not a single meeting generated any revenues for the business but wasted hundreds of hours of my life.

D) Hiring smart people doesn't work if you aren't smart. Everything ultimately comes from the top down.

E) Spending a lot of money on branding is a waste of money for a startup. If you don't know who you are, no amount of money will create materials explaining it.

F) Don't turn down Henry Kravis's five million. It doesn't matter how badly you get diluted. If you have to raise money, take in every dime you can.

G) MOST IMPORTANT: If you raise $30 million, spend none of it. With $30 million we could've stayed in business for 20 years or more and eventually figured ourselves out. Instead, I spent $40 million in the first month or so. I learned a lot, and over $100 million was lost.

EVENTUALLY VAULTUS (THE NAME OF THE COMPANY – I THINK I FORGOT TO MENTION IT UNTIL NOW) WAS SOLD TO ANTENNA SOFTWARE. I MADE NO MONEY, AS I RIGHTFULLY SHOULDN'T.

FOUR YEARS LATER, I WAS ON A TRAIN TO BOSTON WITH MY BUSINESS PARTNER. HE WAS READING BLOOMBERG MAGAZINE.

HOLY SHIT! LOOK AT THIS!

TURNS OUT HE HAD A FRONT CORPORATION THAT WAS MAKING VARIOUS INVESTMENTS FOR HIM FROM THE MONEY HE HAD SOMEHOW MADE OFF OF THE PLO. HIS LARGEST (OR SECOND LARGEST) INVESTMENT WAS TWO MILLION DOLLARS HE HAD PUT INTO A "NEW YORK COMPANY, VAULTUS, INC." I CAN TELL YOU FOR A FACT HIS ESTATE LOST THAT TWO MILLION.

Yasser Arafat 1929-2004

SO, AS THEY SAY IN BROOKLYN, IT WAS GOOD FOR THE JEWS.

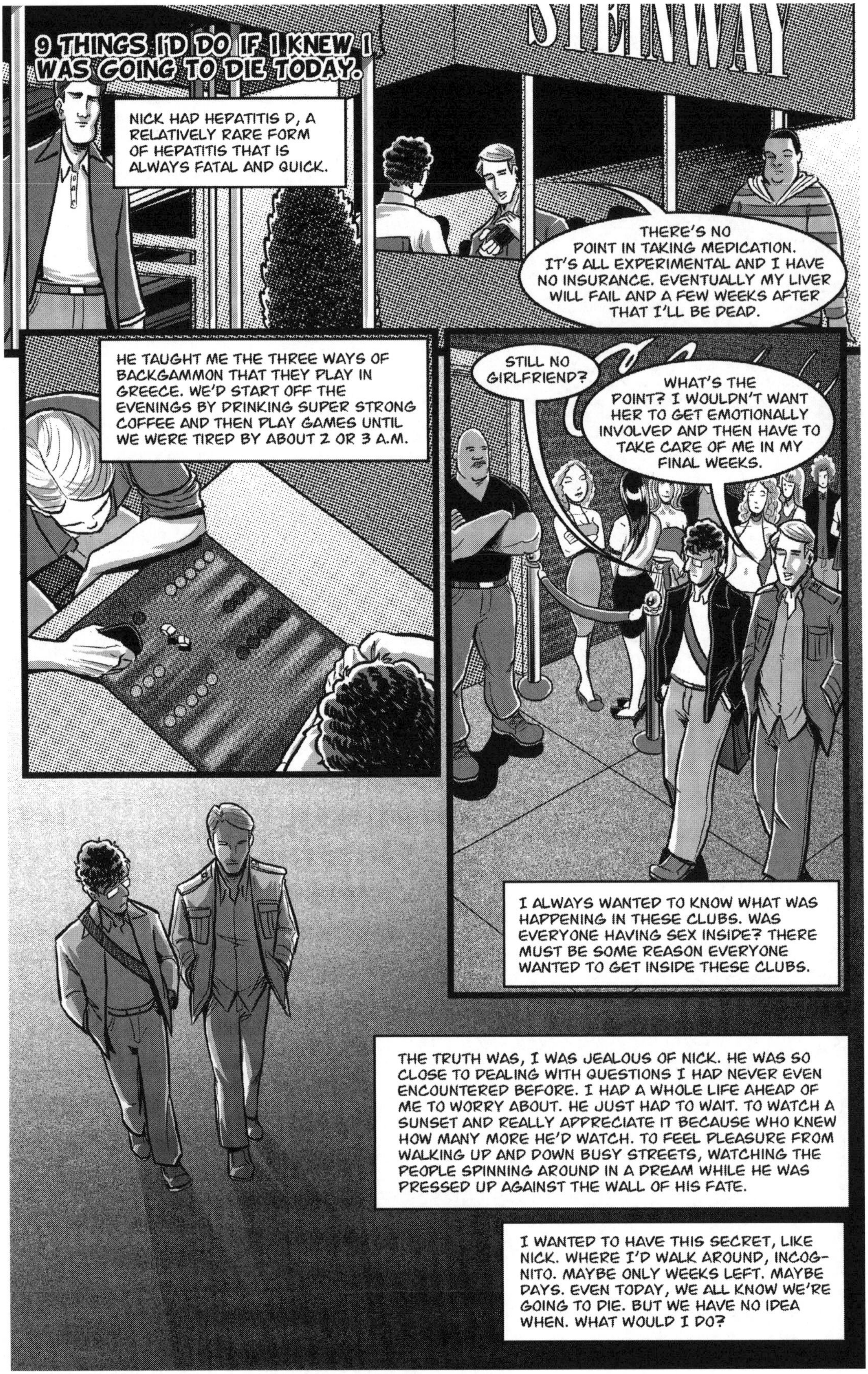
9 THINGS I'D DO IF I KNEW I WAS GOING TO DIE TODAY.
STEINWAY
NICK HAD HEPATITIS D, A RELATIVELY RARE FORM OF HEPATITIS THAT IS ALWAYS FATAL AND QUICK.
THERE'S NO POINT IN TAKING MEDICATION. IT'S ALL EXPERIMENTAL AND I HAVE NO INSURANCE. EVENTUALLY MY LIVER WILL FAIL AND A FEW WEEKS AFTER THAT I'LL BE DEAD.
HE TAUGHT ME THE THREE WAYS OF BACKGAMMON THAT THEY PLAY IN GREECE. WE'D START OFF THE EVENINGS BY DRINKING SUPER STRONG COFFEE AND THEN PLAY GAMES UNTIL WE WERE TIRED BY ABOUT 2 OR 3 A.M.
STILL NO GIRLFRIEND?
WHAT'S THE POINT? I WOULDN'T WANT HER TO GET EMOTIONALLY INVOLVED AND THEN HAVE TO TAKE CARE OF ME IN MY FINAL WEEKS.
I ALWAYS WANTED TO KNOW WHAT WAS HAPPENING IN THESE CLUBS. WAS EVERYONE HAVING SEX INSIDE? THERE MUST BE SOME REASON EVERYONE WANTED TO GET INSIDE THESE CLUBS.
THE TRUTH WAS, I WAS JEALOUS OF NICK. HE WAS SO CLOSE TO DEALING WITH QUESTIONS I HAD NEVER EVEN ENCOUNTERED BEFORE. I HAD A WHOLE LIFE AHEAD OF ME TO WORRY ABOUT. HE JUST HAD TO WAIT. TO WATCH A SUNSET AND REALLY APPRECIATE IT BECAUSE WHO KNEW HOW MANY MORE HE'D WATCH. TO FEEL PLEASURE FROM WALKING UP AND DOWN BUSY STREETS, WATCHING THE PEOPLE SPINNING AROUND IN A DREAM WHILE HE WAS PRESSED UP AGAINST THE WALL OF HIS FATE.
I WANTED TO HAVE THIS SECRET, LIKE NICK. WHERE I'D WALK AROUND, INCOG-NITO. MAYBE ONLY WEEKS LEFT. MAYBE DAYS. EVEN TODAY, WE ALL KNOW WE'RE GOING TO DIE. BUT WE HAVE NO IDEA WHEN. WHAT WOULD I DO?

I CERTAINLY WOULDN'T RETURN ANY PHONE CALLS TO PEOPLE I DON'T WANT TO TALK TO. THAT'S OVER. NOR WOULD I VISIT ANYONE I DIDN'T WANT TO VISIT OR HAVE ANY MEETINGS I DIDN'T NEED TO GO TO, ETC.

SOMETIMES MY KIDS TRY TO TELL ME A STORY AND IT'S HARD TO PAY ATTENTION TO WHAT THEY ARE REALLY SAYING. THEY PACE BACK AND FORTH, AND THE STORY IS HALF IN THEIR MINDS, HALF IN THEIR WORDS SPEWING OUT OF THEM. IT'S HARD TO PAY ATTENTION TO THEM. I'D FIGURE IT ALL OUT THIS ONE TIME.

I WOULDN'T SURF THE WEB. I ALREADY KNOW WAY TOO MUCH ABOUT KIM KARDASHIAN.

WHEN I TRY AND PICTURE WHAT IT WOULD BE LIKE IF I KNEW I WAS GOING TO DIE TODAY, I IMAGINE MYSELF BREATHING VERY DEEPLY THROUGHOUT THE DAY. MOST OF THE TIME WE TAKE VERY SHORT BREATHS. IT'S LIKE A MINI VERSION OF HUFFING AND PUFFING AFTER A RUN, EXCEPT WE DO IT ALL DAY LONG. IF I KNEW TODAY WAS "THE DAY" I THINK I'D TAKE LOTS OF DEEP BREATHS. I DON'T KNOW WHY THIS SEEMS IMPORTANT TO ME.

I'D EMPTY ALL OF MY POCKETS FOR THE ENTIRE DAY. I HAVE A TON OF STUFF IN MY POCKETS RIGHT NOW. WHEN I CHANGE A PAIR OF PANTS I JUST MOVE ALL THIS JUNK FROM ONE PAIR OF PANTS TO THE OTHER. I WANT TO HAVE EMPTY POCKETS THE DAY I DIE.

I THINK I WOULD BE KIND TO PEOPLE. I DON'T THINK I WOULD FEEL THE URGE TO TELL ANYONE OFF WHO HAS WRONGED ME IN THE PAST. MOST OF THESE PEOPLE ALREADY KNOW HOW I FEEL ABOUT THEM ANYWAY. I'D WANT TO MAKE SURE THAT I WAS KIND TO ENOUGH PEOPLE SO THAT AFTER I WAS GONE PEOPLE WOULD REMEMBER FOREVER THAT LAST MOMENT OF KINDNESS. IT WOULD BE A MEMORY FOREVER SINCE EVERYONE TAKES A MENTAL SNAPSHOT OF THE LAST MOMENT THEY SAW SOMEONE.

You always had really nice hair

I'D PROBABLY WANT TO AT LEAST WRITE EMAILS TO EVERYONE I WANTED TO SAY GOODBYE TO. BUT I WOULDN'T SAY GOODBYE. THAT'S TOO SAD. INSTEAD I'D WRITE PEOPLE A LIST OF ALL THE REASONS I LIKED THEM. IT WOULD BE SOMEWHAT EMBARRASSING BUT WHY SHOULD I CARE?

I'D WANT TO BE CLEAN FOR THE DAY, AND HAPPY WITH HOW I LOOKED. I MEAN, WHAT'S GOING TO CHANGE NOW?

SOAP

I'D SPEND AS MUCH OF THE DAY AS POSSIBLE WITH MY WIFE. I SELFISHLY WOULD WANT HER TO FEEL SAD AFTER I DIED SO I'D NEED TO LEAVE HER WITH SOME GOOD MEMORIES.

LIVE TODAY LIKE IT'S YOUR LAST.

STOP WORRYING ABOUT ALL THE USUAL WORRIES. SEND EMAILS TO ALL THE PEOPLE YOU LIKE, LISTING THEIR FAVORABLE ATTRIBUTES. OR AT LEAST SOME OF THEM. EVERY DAY I COULD DO ALL THE THINGS ON THE ABOVE LIST. IT'S A GOOD THOUGHT. BUT IT'S HARD TO DO IN PRACTICE WHILE WE ARE LIVING THE DREAM.

I MOVED OUT OF ASTORIA WHEN I STARTED MAKING MORE MONEY. I WAS NEVER GOOD AT GOODBYES SO I JUST PACKED UP AND LEFT WITHOUT TALKING TO ANY OF THE PEOPLE I HAD BECOME FRIENDS WITH IN THE EIGHT MONTHS I LIVED THERE. A FEW YEARS LATER I RAN INTO NICK ON THE STREET IN MANHAT-TAN. I'M ASHAMED TO ADMIT I WAS KIND OF DISAPPOINTED HE WASN'T DEAD YET. LIKE MAYBE HE HAD LIED TO ME.

MAYBE HE WAS THINKING THE SAME THING ABOUT ME.

THE-ONE-REASON WHY FACEBOOK IS WORTH $50 BILLION

IN SEVENTH GRADE THE BIGGER KIDS WOULD JUST RANDOMLY PUNCH YOU RIGHT IN THE FACE AND LAUGH. KIDS GOT CRUEL. BUT IN FIFTH GRADE IT WAS ALL ABOUT JUDY BLUME. KIDS HAD CRUSHES FOR THE FIRST TIME BUT NOBODY CALLED IT CRUSHES. IT WAS "LOVE." THEY WONDERED ABOUT GOD AND SEX AND WHAT THE OLDER KIDS DID.

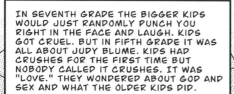

LEE APPLEBAUM, ON MY HEBREW SCHOOL CARPOOL, TOLD MY MOM, ME, AND JENNIFER F., THAT HIS BABYSITTER PEED IN HIS GIRLFRIEND'S MOUTH.

THAT WAS THE MOST DISGUSTING THING I EVER HEARD.

IN FIFTH GRADE, AFTER THREE MONTHS OF PRETENDING TO ENJOY HOPSCOTCH WITH THE GIRLS RATHER THAN KICKBALL WITH THE GUYS DURING RECESS, I FINALLY HAD ENOUGH COURAGE TO TELL BETH THAT MAYBE POSSIBLY I HAD REAL FEELINGS FOR HER.

I CAN'T REMEMBER WHAT HAPPENED AFTER THAT. EVERYONE WAS EMBARRASSED. SHE WAS. I WAS. ALL OF OUR FRIENDS WERE. SOME RUNNING AWAY OCCURRED. BUT A FEW WEEKS LATER WE STARTED RIDING OUR BIKES TOGETHER AFTER SCHOOL.

AND THEN I STARTED FINDING OUT CERTAIN THINGS ABOUT MYSELF THAT I NEVER KNEW BEFORE BUT I WOULD KNOW ALL TOO WELL FOR YEARS AFTER.

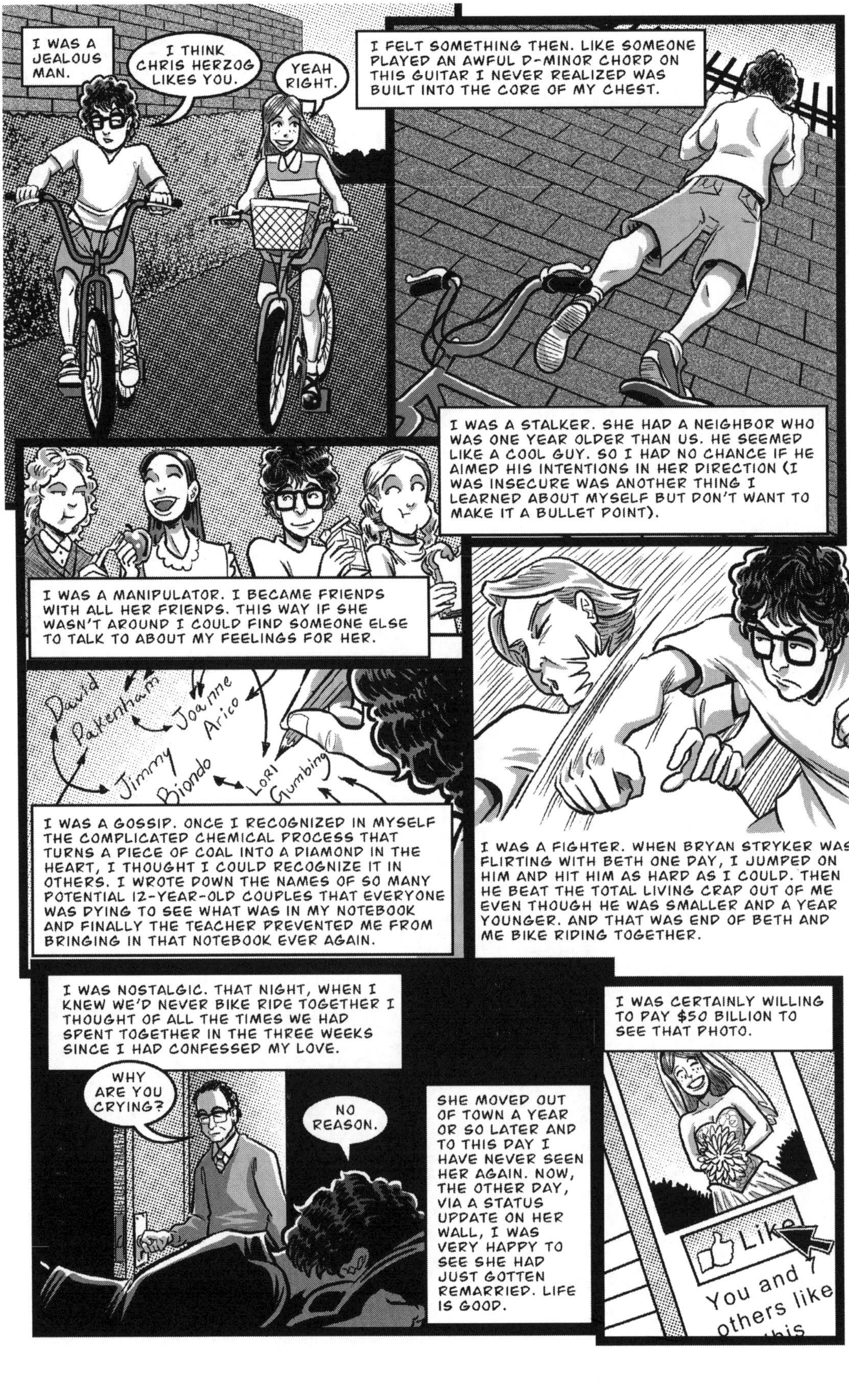
I WAS A JEALOUS MAN.
I THINK CHRIS HERZOG LIKES YOU.
YEAH RIGHT.
I FELT SOMETHING THEN. LIKE SOMEONE PLAYED AN AWFUL D-MINOR CHORD ON THIS GUITAR I NEVER REALIZED WAS BUILT INTO THE CORE OF MY CHEST.
I WAS A STALKER. SHE HAD A NEIGHBOR WHO WAS ONE YEAR OLDER THAN US. HE SEEMED LIKE A COOL GUY. SO I HAD NO CHANCE IF HE AIMED HIS INTENTIONS IN HER DIRECTION (I WAS INSECURE WAS ANOTHER THING I LEARNED ABOUT MYSELF BUT DON'T WANT TO MAKE IT A BULLET POINT).
I WAS A MANIPULATOR. I BECAME FRIENDS WITH ALL HER FRIENDS. THIS WAY IF SHE WASN'T AROUND I COULD FIND SOMEONE ELSE TO TALK TO ABOUT MY FEELINGS FOR HER.
David Pakenham
Joanne Arico
Jimmy Biondo
Lori Gumbing
I WAS A GOSSIP. ONCE I RECOGNIZED IN MYSELF THE COMPLICATED CHEMICAL PROCESS THAT TURNS A PIECE OF COAL INTO A DIAMOND IN THE HEART, I THOUGHT I COULD RECOGNIZE IT IN OTHERS. I WROTE DOWN THE NAMES OF SO MANY POTENTIAL 12-YEAR-OLD COUPLES THAT EVERYONE WAS DYING TO SEE WHAT WAS IN MY NOTEBOOK AND FINALLY THE TEACHER PREVENTED ME FROM BRINGING IN THAT NOTEBOOK EVER AGAIN.
I WAS A FIGHTER. WHEN BRYAN STRYKER WAS FLIRTING WITH BETH ONE DAY, I JUMPED ON HIM AND HIT HIM AS HARD AS I COULD. THEN HE BEAT THE TOTAL LIVING CRAP OUT OF ME EVEN THOUGH HE WAS SMALLER AND A YEAR YOUNGER. AND THAT WAS END OF BETH AND ME BIKE RIDING TOGETHER.
I WAS NOSTALGIC. THAT NIGHT, WHEN I KNEW WE'D NEVER BIKE RIDE TOGETHER I THOUGHT OF ALL THE TIMES WE HAD SPENT TOGETHER IN THE THREE WEEKS SINCE I HAD CONFESSED MY LOVE.
WHY ARE YOU CRYING?
NO REASON.
SHE MOVED OUT OF TOWN A YEAR OR SO LATER AND TO THIS DAY I HAVE NEVER SEEN HER AGAIN. NOW, THE OTHER DAY, VIA A STATUS UPDATE ON HER WALL, I WAS VERY HAPPY TO SEE SHE HAD JUST GOTTEN REMARRIED. LIFE IS GOOD.
I WAS CERTAINLY WILLING TO PAY $50 BILLION TO SEE THAT PHOTO.
Like
You and 7 others like

THE MOMENT BEFORE ABBEY ROAD

THE MOMENT BEFORE THEIR FAMOUS WALK ACROSS ABBEY ROAD, PAUL HAD TO ADJUST SOMETHING ON RINGO'S COLLAR. AT THAT MOMENT THEY WERE HUMAN. IN THE FAMOUS WALK, WHICH WE'VE SEEN EVERYWHERE, THEY AREN'T HUMAN ANYMORE. THEY'VE BECOME GODS.

BETWEEN THE TIME I WAS SEPARATED FROM MY EX-WIFE AND THE TIME I MET MY CURRENT WIFE, I WORKED VERY HARD TO FIGHT LONELINESS. IT WAS A FULLTIME JOB FOR ME.

E-LUV.COM

THREE HOURS A DAY AT LEAST.

MEETING PEOPLE FOR SOMEONE NATURALLY SHY LIKE ME REQUIRES INTENSIVE WORK. I WOULD TALK TO WOMEN IN THE STREET. ASK OUT PEOPLE I MET IN ELEVATORS. HECK, I EVEN CREATED MY OWN DATING SERVICE I WAS SO OBSESSED WITH DATING. THE ARCHAEOLOGICAL REMAINS ARE STILL AROUND FOR MY FAILED DATING SERVICE, 14OLOVE.COM.

IN ANY CASE, I NEEDED TO DO SOME HOMEWORK THIS ONE PARTICULAR EVENING.

NATIONALITY
British

OCCUPATION
Singer

INTERESTS
Kabbalah

Research Kabbalah for Thurs.

SO I WENT OUT TO MY FAVORITE BOOKSTORE AND SPENT THE ENTIRE AFTERNOON LOOKING AT BOOKS BY PHILIP BERG AND HIS SON (OR HIS FATHER, I FORGET - "THE BERGS").

I COULD PICK UP RELIGIONS AS EASILY AS I USED TO PICK UP PROGRAMMING LANGUAGES.

WE WERE JUST GOING FOR THE DESSERTS (DON'T WASTE MORE TIME THAN YOU HAVE TO) AND, PRESUMABLY, ALCOHOL. AND SHE GAVE ME HER DEBUT ALBUM AND I LOST IT WITHOUT LISTENING TO IT.

I HAD INTENDED TO LISTEN TO IT BUT SOMETIMES YOU JUST LOSE THINGS.

Klak

I DIDN'T KNOW YOU WERE THAT INTO KABBALAH.

IT MAKES A LOT OF SENSE TO ME.

YOU SHOULD GO TO THE CLASSES WITH ME. WE CAN STUDY TOGETHER.

WHY THE HELL NOT? THE WORLD IS A LITTLE BIT OFF-KILTER. GOD PUT IT ON ITS COURSE BUT WE HIT SOMETHING. WE RAN SMACK INTO THE MOON. BUT NOW THE EARTH IS OFF-COURSE. IT CAN'T RETURN. ANYTHING WE CAN DO TO MAKE IT RIGHT SEEMS OK TO ME.

LATER THAT MONTH I WOULD MEET SOMEONE IN A TEA HOUSE. BUT I DIDN'T KNOW THAT THEN AND THAT'S ANOTHER STORY.

THEN, SITTING IN THE MANDARIN HOTEL, EATING DESSERTS, AND TALKING TO A BRITISH SINGER ABOUT THE ESOTERIC RECESSES OF JUDAISM WRITTEN BY MADONNA'S GURU, I WAS IN THE MOMENT BEFORE THE MOMENT.

PREPARE BETTER THAN THE NEXT PERSON. WAKE UP 15 MINUTES EARLIER THAN EVERYONE ELSE. READ A LITTLE BIT MORE. CLEAN THAT EXTRA THREAD HANGING OFF YOUR PANTS. WRITE THE BEST POST YOU CAN BEFORE YOU HIT PUBLISH. SEND THOSE FIRST FEW E-MAILS TO FLIRT, TO ENTICE, AND THEN CONFIRM A FIRST DATE.

Dummies Guide To KABALLA

THE OUTCOMES ARE ALL UNCERTAIN. LIFE HASN'T CHANGED JUST YET. YOU CAN BE ANXIOUS FOR THE OUTCOME. OR YOU CAN RELISH THE MOMENT, KNOWING THE PREPARATION AND YOUR DAILY PRACTICE IS IN PLACE. YOU'VE DONE ALL YOU CAN. IT'S THE MOMENT BEFORE THE MOMENT. GOOD THINGS WILL HAPPEN.

NOW YOU HAVE TO WAIT. IF YOU DID THE RIGHT PREP-ARATION, THE MOMENT WILL COME. IF YOU DID THE PREPA-RATION WITH PASSION, WITH INSPIRATION, WITH ASPIRATION. NOW YOU WAIT.

FUTURE WIFE

EVERY DAY WE HAVE THE POTEN-TIAL FOR GODHOOD, TO BE SOMETHING THAT BREAKS US OUT OF THAT FATE. THAT CAREENS US ONTO A PATH GOD HAD NOT INTENDED FOR US.

IMAGINE YOU ARE PAUL MCARTNEY RIGHT THIS SECOND. YOU'RE ADJUSTING RINGO'S COLLAR ON HIS TUXEDO. THE NOON SUN IS HOT AND BRIGHT AND YOU'RE UNCOMFORTABLE IN THE CLOTHES BUT EVERY WRINKLE HAS TO BE JUST RIGHT. YOU'RE ABOUT TO CROSS THE STREET TO MAKE THE FAMOUS PHOTO FOR ABBEY ROAD.

AND FOR THE LAST TIME IN YOUR LIFE, YOU ARE 100% HUMAN.

WHAT IT FEELS LIKE TO BE RICH

SOLD

IT'S BEEN A DECADE SINCE THEN AND A LOT HAS HAPPENED. SOMEONE ON QUORA YESTERDAY ASKED THE QUESTION:

Quora | Find Questions, Topics and People | Add Question

What does it feel like to be rich? ✎ Edit
Add Comment • Add Follow-Up Question • Flag Questio

9 Answers • Create Answer Summary

2rich4u
Better than being poor.

BIGmonee$
I was finally able to buy a Porsche.

Scrooge McDuck
I'll always remember how I made my lucky #1 dime...

Richie Rich
I like to share my money with other children.

Charles Montgomery Burns
What good is money if you can't inspire terror in your fellow man?

Jed Clampett
Well shucks, I reckon it ain't that

I FIGURED I'D ANSWER BASED ON MY PRE-2000 EXPERIENCES. I'LL SAVE 2000-2010 FOR ANOTHER TIME.

AFTER LOSING OVER ONE MILLION A WEEK, CASH, FOR THE ENTIRE SUMMER OF 2000, I WAS FORCED TO SELL MY APARTMENT. MY SELF-ESTEEM WAS GONE, MY APARTMENT WAS GONE, AND I HADN'T SLEPT A FULL NIGHT IN ALMOST THREE YEARS.

MONEY WAS NEVER ABOUT THAT FOR ME, THEN OR NOW. THERE'S NEVER BEEN ANYTHING I WANTED TO BUY (OTHER THAN THE NEXT IPAD!). I HAVE MINIMAL MATERIAL POSSESSIONS.

IF YOU KNOW ME YOU'D SEE I DRESS LIKE CRAP AND THE EDGES OF ALL OF MY PANTS ARE FRAYED. I DON'T OWN A SUIT.

I DON'T HAVE A DRIVER'S LICENSE SO FANCY CARS ARE OUT. I LIKE COMIC BOOKS MORE THAN PAINTINGS. I DON'T LIKE TO FLY OR SAIL. AND I DON'T DRINK WINE OR EAT OUT A LOT. SO WHAT DID IT MEAN FOR ME BACK THEN...

DNA:
I FINALLY FELT GOOD ENOUGH ABOUT MYSELF TO PASS ON MY GENES AND HAVE CHILDREN. I HAD NEVER FELT THAT BEFORE BUT SOMEHOW HAVING A SIGNIFICANT AMOUNT OF MONEY GAVE ME PERMISSION TO WANT TO HAVE KIDS.

SAFETY:
FOR THE BRIEFEST OF MOMENTS, I FELT "SAFE" - LIKE NOTHING COULD HARM ME AND I COULD LIVE FOREVER. IN 1999, I VISITED THE CHAIRMAN OF A COMPANY FOR WHICH I WAS A SHAREHOLDER.

I DON'T EVEN HAVE TO DO THIS ANYMORE. I HAVE SO MUCH MONEY NOW THAT NOTHING CAN TOUCH ME.

I KNOW IT SOUNDS UNBELIEVABLE AND A CLICHE BUT A YEAR LATER HE CAME DOWN WITH CANCER. MONEY HAS ITS BENEFITS. IMMORTALITY IS NOT ONE OF THEM.

ANOTHER EXAMPLE: A FRIEND OF MINE WAS RUNNING A PROMINENT GAMING SITE AND WANTED TO SELL. I INTRODUCED HIM TO A SUCCESSFUL GUY I KNEW ON WALL STREET. MY FRIEND AND I SAT THERE WHILE SHLOMO (NOT HIS REAL NAME, BUT YOU GET THE DRIFT) SAID:

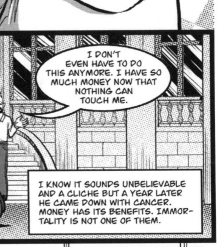

LOOK AT ME! TEN YEARS AGO I WAS A SCHLUB. NOW I HAVE $100 MILLION!

ABOUT TWO YEARS LATER SHLOMO WAS IN THE CENTER OF A MASSIVE FBI STING INVOLVING A CURRENCY BROKERAGE HE HAD STARTED THAT HAD BEEN POCKETING INVESTORS' MONEY SINCE THE 70'S.

SCARCITY: MY FEELINGS OF SAFETY AND IMMORTALITY QUICKLY GAVE WAY TO SCARCITY. AFTER ALL, I THOUGHT, IF I COULD MAKE $10 MILLION THEN IT MUST BE TOO EASY.

MAN, EVERYBODY'S GOT $10 MILLION THESE DAYS.

NOT EVERYONE...

FRIENDS:
I LOST SOME. THEN I MADE SOME NEW ONES. BY THE TIME I WAS GOING DOWN IN THE ELEVATOR FROM MY APARTMENT THE LAST TIME, 100% OF THOSE NEW FRIENDS WERE DESTINED TO NEVER SPEAK TO ME AGAIN.

THE VALUE OF MONEY. I REALIZED (TOO LATE THEN, BUT I LEARNED) THAT I NEVER KNEW THE VALUE OF MONEY. I HAD NEVER EVEN BEEN AWARE OF MONEY BEFORE. NOW MY ONLY GOAL WAS MONEY, MONEY, MONEY, AND MORE MONEY.

IT'S LIKE LOSING A LOVED ONE!

SWEETIE, SOUNDS LIKE YOU'VE NEVER REALLY LOST A LOVED ONE BEFORE.

MONEY IS A GREAT THING. IT'S THE PAYOFF ON HARD WORK, GREAT LUCK (WHICH IS OFTEN EARNED LUCK) AND YOU CAN DO AMAZING THINGS WITH IT. VERY FEW THINGS ARE BETTER THAN EARNING A LOT OF MONEY.

BUT MONEY FINDS A HOME ONLY IN PLACES WHERE IT'S APPRECIATED. I DIDN'T APPRECIATE THE MONEY. SO IT LEFT ME.

I WANTED TO CRY I FELT SO BAD ABOUT WHAT WAS HAPPENING. BUT IT WAS TOO MUCH TO THINK ABOUT.

SO FOR A BRIEF MOMENT I WATCHED THE SNOW AND RE- MEMBERED WHAT IT WAS LIKE TO BE A KID. TASTING THE FIRST SNOW OF THE YEAR ON THE TIP OF MY TONGUE.

17

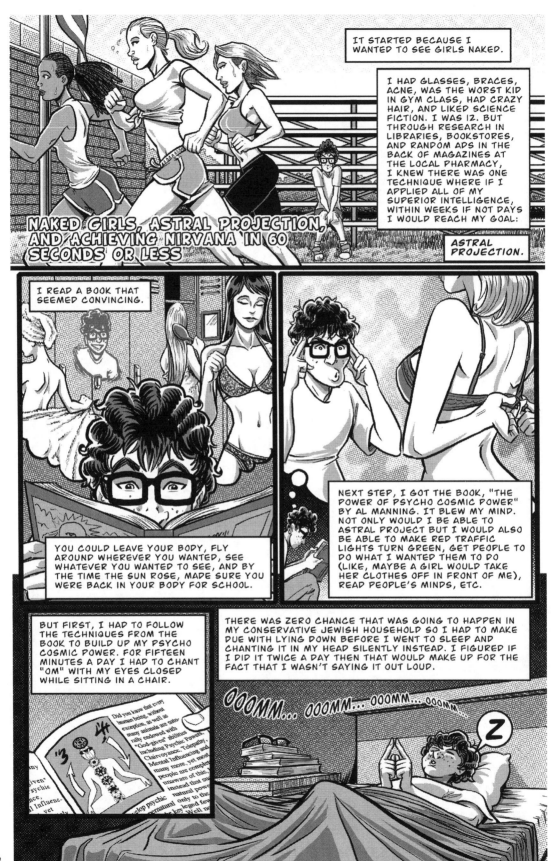

IT STARTED BECAUSE I WANTED TO SEE GIRLS NAKED.

I HAD GLASSES, BRACES, ACNE, WAS THE WORST KID IN GYM CLASS, HAD CRAZY HAIR, AND LIKED SCIENCE FICTION. I WAS 12. BUT THROUGH RESEARCH IN LIBRARIES, BOOKSTORES, AND RANDOM ADS IN THE BACK OF MAGAZINES AT THE LOCAL PHARMACY, I KNEW THERE WAS ONE TECHNIQUE WHERE IF I APPLIED ALL OF MY SUPERIOR INTELLIGENCE, WITHIN WEEKS IF NOT DAYS I WOULD REACH MY GOAL: ASTRAL PROJECTION.

NAKED GIRLS, ASTRAL PROJECTION, AND ACHIEVING NIRVANA IN 60 SECONDS OR LESS

I READ A BOOK THAT SEEMED CONVINCING.

YOU COULD LEAVE YOUR BODY, FLY AROUND WHEREVER YOU WANTED, SEE WHATEVER YOU WANTED TO SEE, AND BY THE TIME THE SUN ROSE, MADE SURE YOU WERE BACK IN YOUR BODY FOR SCHOOL.

NEXT STEP, I GOT THE BOOK, "THE POWER OF PSYCHO COSMIC POWER" BY AL MANNING. IT BLEW MY MIND. NOT ONLY WOULD I BE ABLE TO ASTRAL PROJECT BUT I WOULD ALSO BE ABLE TO MAKE RED TRAFFIC LIGHTS TURN GREEN, GET PEOPLE TO DO WHAT I WANTED THEM TO DO (LIKE, MAYBE A GIRL WOULD TAKE HER CLOTHES OFF IN FRONT OF ME), READ PEOPLE'S MINDS, ETC.

BUT FIRST, I HAD TO FOLLOW THE TECHNIQUES FROM THE BOOK TO BUILD UP MY PSYCHO COSMIC POWER. FOR FIFTEEN MINUTES A DAY I HAD TO CHANT "OM" WITH MY EYES CLOSED WHILE SITTING IN A CHAIR.

THERE WAS ZERO CHANCE THAT WAS GOING TO HAPPEN IN MY CONSERVATIVE JEWISH HOUSEHOLD SO I HAD TO MAKE DUE WITH LYING DOWN BEFORE I WENT TO SLEEP AND CHANTING IT IN MY HEAD INSTEAD. I FIGURED IF I DID IT TWICE A DAY THEN THAT WOULD MAKE UP FOR THE FACT THAT I WASN'T SAYING IT OUT LOUD.

OOOMM... OOOMM... OOOMM... OOOMM...

Z

WHEN IT DIDN'T WORK, I INCREASED THE TIME TO 30 MINUTES A DAY, TWICE A DAY. I SET MY ALARM CLOCK FOR 4:50 A.M. SO I WOULD BE DONE DOING MY VERY NON-JEWISH THINGS BEFORE MY PARENTS WOKE UP. IT DIDN'T WORK. I TRIED OUT SOME TECHNIQUES IN ANOTHER BOOK, "SECRETS OF THE MYSTIC MASTERS," BUT THAT DIDN'T WORK EITHER. I DID MORE RESEARCH. OTHER TECHNIQUES.

I FOUND OUT THERE WERE OTHER PEOPLE DOING THIS TYPE OF ACTIVITY SO I STARTED READING BOOKS ABOUT BUDDHISM, TAOISM, HINDUISM, ALL THE TIME HIDING THEM FROM MY PARENTS. NOT EVEN THE RABBI SUSPECTED.

BEFORE LONG I WAS MEDITATING ON A DAILY BASIS, MY NEW GOAL TO ACHIEVE SOME SORT OF ETERNAL HAPPINESS (ALAS, IT WOULD BE ABOUT SIX MORE YEARS BEFORE MY INITIAL GOAL WAS ACHIEVED). IT BECAME MORE OR LESS, A CONSISTENT (OR RATHER, DRASTI-CALLY INCONSISTENT) PART OF MY LIFE.

EVERYBODY HAS AN ONGOING DIALOGUE RUNNING IN THEIR HEAD ALL DAY LONG CONSISTING OF ALL THE THINGS THEY ARE WORKING ON, ALL THE THINGS THEY ARE AFRAID OF, ALL OF THE THINGS THAT BOTHER THEM, ALL THE PLANS AND MACHINATIONS THEY ARE IN THE MIDDLE OF, ETC.

MEDITATION HELPS BREAK OUT OF THAT FOR A FEW SECONDS AT A TIME SO YOU CAN SEE IT FOR WHAT IT ALL IS. NOTHING. AT LEAST, NOTHING YOU SHOULD WASTE HUNDREDS OF HOURS OF YOUR LIFE OBSESSING ON.

BUT, AGAIN, IT'S UNREALIS-TIC TO EXPECT PEOPLE TO SPEND 20 MINUTES, TWICE A DAY, TO "PRACTICE" THIS ABILITY TO DETACH. PEOPLE CAN'T SIT STILL. I CAN'T.

I THINK THE IDEA OF MEDITATING FOR SO LONG IS A MORE EASTERN WORLD CONCEPT. HERE'S THE WESTERN VERSION. IT'S JUST LIKE DIETING. INSTEAD OF HAVING 2 OR 3 HUGE MEALS A DAY, WHY NOT BREAK IT DOWN INTO 6 SMALLER MEALS SPACED THROUGHOUT THE DAY. OR 10 SMALLER MEALS? PERSONALLY, I THINK IF YOU DO A 60 SECOND MEDITATION, 10 TO 20 TIMES A DAY, BUDDHA WOULD APPROVE.

HERE'S SOME 60 SECOND MEDITATIONS YOU CAN PRACTICE.

ELEVATOR: IN AN ELEVATOR FILLED WITH PEOPLE, TAKE A DEEP BREATH, FEEL YOUR ANXIETY AT NOT BEING ABLE TO LOOK AT YOUR BLACKBERRY (EVERYONE ELSE ON THE ELEVATOR IS LOOKING AT THEIRS EVEN THOUGH THERE IS NO RECEPTION). WHERE IS THE ANXIETY BEING FELT ON YOUR BODY? HOW MANY DEEP BREATHS CAN YOU DO BEFORE THE ELEVATOR REACHES ITS DESTINATION?

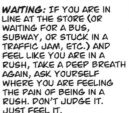

WAITING: IF YOU ARE IN LINE AT THE STORE (OR WAITING FOR A BUS, SUBWAY, OR STUCK IN A TRAFFIC JAM, ETC.) AND FEEL LIKE YOU ARE IN A RUSH, TAKE A DEEP BREATH AGAIN, ASK YOURSELF WHERE YOU ARE FEELING THE PAIN OF BEING IN A RUSH. DON'T JUDGE IT. JUST FEEL IT.

IF YOU HAPPEN TO FIGURE OUT HOW TO ASTRAL PROJECT WHILE YOU ARE DOING THIS, PLEASE CALL ME.

DISHES: STOP YOURSELF FROM DAYDREAMING. REALLY TRY TO DO A GOOD JOB WASHING EACH DISH. NOT A SPECK ON THEM. FOCUS! YOU JUST MISSED A SPOT! YOUR ONLY PURPOSE IN LIFE IS TO WASH THE ONE DISH YOU ARE CURRENTLY WORKING ON.

OH BOY...

ALIEN: IMAGINE THAT YOU ARE AN ALIEN FROM OUTERSPACE AND YOU WERE JUST TRANSPORTED INTO THIS BODY ("QUANTUM LEAP" STYLE). YOU HAVE NO IDEA WHO YOU ARE AND YOU HAVE TO START WITH A COMPLETELY BLANK SLATE. SPEND THE NEXT MINUTE FIGURING IT OUT. "WHO AM I?" "WHERE AM I?" "WHO ARE THESE PEOPLE AROUND ME?" FIGURE IT OUT.

♥ LIST
Claudia
Molly
Josie

WAKING: WHEN YOU WAKE UP, TAKE THREE DEEP BREATHS, COUNT THEM. TRY TO LIST ALL OF THE THINGS YOU HEAR THAT MOMENT. DO YOU HEAR CARS OUTSIDE? BIRDS? YOUR HOUSE CREAKING? KIDS DOWNSTAIRS?

GRATITUDE: MAKE A LIST IN YOUR HEAD OF ALL THE PEOPLE IN YOUR LIFE YOU ARE GRATEFUL FOR. ONLY TAKES A FEW MINUTES, DRASTICALLY REDUCES STRESS.

SURRENDER: SPEND SIXTY SECONDS COMPLETELY DEDICATING THIS DAY TO WHATEVER HIGHER POWER YOU WANT TO BELIEVE IN (THE FORCE, GOD, THE TAO, THE SUPREME ALIEN INTELLIGENCE FROM THE BLACK HOLE THAT'S AT THE CENTER OF THE MILKY WAY GALAXY, ETC) THEY ARE GOING TO TAKE OVER YOUR BODY AND MIND AND DO THEIR THING TODAY.

TENSE: TENSE EVERY MUSCLE IN YOUR BODY FOR 5 SECONDS. TENSE AS MUCH AS YOU CAN. THEN RELAX. FEELS BETTER, RIGHT?

HATE: THINK OF ONE PERSON YOU REALLY HATE. NOW, TRULY AND SINCERELY WISH HIM THE BEST IN YOUR HEAD. THIS PERSON IS JUST TRYING TO GET THROUGH LIFE ALSO. MAYBE THEY'VE LOST SOME MONEY, OR MAYBE THEY ARE LONELY. BUT THERE IS SOME SUFFERING THAT CAUSED THEM TO DO THE THINGS THEY DID. EVERYONE IS SUFFERING. WISH THEM THE BEST.

WALKING: WHEN YOU ARE WALKING AROUND IN THE CITY, IF YOU ARE ANYTHING LIKE ME YOU PROBABLY HATE MOST OF THE PEOPLE WHO YOU PASS, EVEN IF YOU DON'T KNOW THEM OR HAVE NEVER SEEN THEM BEFORE. CATCH YOURSELF DOING THAT. TRY THE REVERSE. TRY LIKING ALL OF THEM. NOT IN A PATRONIZING WAY. BUT TRY TO REALLY LIKE THEM.

THESE ALL WORK AND ARE JUST AS VALID AS THE 6 HOUR MEDITATIONS ANY TIBETAN GURU IS DOING IN HIS CAVE. HECK, IN OUR WORLD WE HAVE THE ADDED ADVANTAGE THAT WE ARE TRULY STRESSED OUT OF OUR MINDS WITH WORK, FAMILY, MORTGAGES, RESPONSIBILITIES.

THIS "PRACTICE" WILL HAVE REAL PRACTICAL RESULTS (ALTHOUGH PROBABLY NOT MY ORIGINAL GOAL FROM BACK WHEN I WAS 12 YEARS OLD).

BREAKDANCING AND MASTER OF THE UNIVERSE

I WANTED TO LEARN HOW TO BREAKDANCE SO I PAID SOME KID $15 TO TEACH ME OUT OF MY HARD-EARNED NEWSPAPER ROUTE MONEY.

MAYBE THE BEST SUMMER OF MY LIFE. CERTAINLY THE MOST EMBARRASSING WHEN I NOW THINK BACK ON IT.

IN EVERY SPARE MOMENT I EITHER HUNG OUT WITH MY NEW FRIENDS, HAVING NO ISSUES ABANDONING MY OTHER FRIENDS WHO WEREN'T COOL ENOUGH TO UNDERSTAND THE FINER SUBTLETIES OF THE WINDMILL, OR I PRACTICED IN FRONT OF A MIRROR. IT'S EMBARRASSING WRITING THESE WORDS DOWN.

OF COURSE, LIKE IN ALL MY REMEMBRANCES, I THOUGHT THAT BY LEARNING HOW TO SPIN ON MY BACK AND DO OTHER RANDOM CONTORTIONS WITH MY BODY I WOULD, OF COURSE, MEET GIRLS IN CLUBS. BUT IT DIDN'T HAPPEN BECAUSE I STILL HAD "ME" TO DEAL WITH. THE ME WHO COULDN'T TALK TO ANYONE OR WAS TOO SHY TO ASK ANYONE FOR THEIR NUMBER.

MUCH LATER, WHEN I APPLIED TO COLLEGES I NEVER MENTIONED THIS LITTLE EPISODE IN MY LIFE.

BUT IT'S ALL RELATED TO MAKING MONEY. MY INSECURITY WAS SO HIGH THAT ONLY BY BEING THE BEST AT SOMETHING COULD I MUSTER THE CONFIDENCE TO SAY, "THIS IS ME, THIS IS WHAT I DO." IF I WANTED TO PURSUE ANYTHING, I HAD TO APPLY THE FOLLOWING PRINCIPLES TO GET GOOD AT A FEW THINGS.

GOOD ENOUGH TO MAKE SOME MONEY, GOOD ENOUGH TO HAVE FUN, GOOD ENOUGH TO HAVE SOME INTERESTING EXPERIENCES ALONG THE WAY.

TEACHER:
GET A TEACHER/MENTOR. I'VE DONE THIS WITH EVERYTHING FROM CHESS, TO STOCK-PICKING, HEDGE FUNDS, ENTREPRENEUR-SHIP, ETC. YOU ABSOLUTELY NEED A TEACHER IN ANYTHING YOU DO TO HELP YOU QUICKLY JUMP OVER THE BASIC MISTAKES.

READ:
READ EVERYTHING YOU CAN. I HAVE OVER 200 BOOKS ABOUT CHESS. I'VE READ OVER 2-300 BOOKS ON INVESTING. 200 BOOKS ON A TOPIC SEEMS TO BE ABOUT THE RIGHT NUMBER. EVERY DAY NEW THINGS ARE DEVELOPING IN YOUR FIELD. IF YOU ARE A LAWYER, YOU NEED TO FOLLOW EVERY CASE. IF YOU'RE A DOCTOR, EVERY NEW BREAKTHROUGH TECHNOLOGY.

HISTORY:
YOU NEED TO KNOW THE HISTORY OF WHAT YOU ARE DOING. IT'S THE ONLY WAY TO UNDERSTAND WHAT IS HAPPENING NOW.

FAIL:
STUDY YOUR MISTAKES. YOU'LL ALWAYS HAVE LOSSES. BUT THE SECOND YOU BLAME IT ON "BAD LUCK" THEN YOU'VE GONE FROM HAVING A LOSS TO BECOMING A LOSER.

IDEAS:
WHEN YOU WORK AT A COMPANY, IT'S NOT ENOUGH THAT YOU BE A GOOD EMPLOYEE. YOU MUST ACTUALLY BECOME THE COMPANY. ONCE YOU INJECT YOUR OWN LIFE FORCE INTO AN ENDEAVOR, THEN YOU INEVITABLY WILL BRING TO IT NEW IDEAS.

DO:
YOU NEED TO NOT JUST READ AND STUDY BUT DO. IF YOU WANT TO WRITE A SCREENPLAY, EVERY DAY YOU NEED TO WRITE. IF YOU WANT TO BE AN ENTREPRENEUR, YOU MUST START RIGHT AWAY THINKING OF SERVICES OR PRODUCTS YOU CAN PROVIDE AND SELL. NOBODY IS GOING TO DO IT FOR YOU.

HOW LONG DOES IT TAKE?
YOU NEED TO BE PATIENT. THREE YEARS BEFORE YOU CAN SAY, "I UNDERSTAND THIS FIELD," FIVE BEFORE YOU CAN SAY "I CAN MAKE A LIVING DOING THIS," AND EIGHT BEFORE YOU CAN SAY, "I'M ONE OF THE BEST IN THE WORLD AT THIS." IT'S OK NOT TO BE THE BEST IN THE WORLD AT SOMETHING.

FINALLY, YOU NEED TO *MAINTAIN.* I'M NOT SAYING I'VE MASTERED ANYTHING. AND I HAVEN'T CREATED BILLIONS IN VALUE. BUT IF YOU THREW OUT A PIECE OF LINOLEUM AND WANTED ME TO SPIN ON MY BACK, I CAN PROBABLY STILL DO THAT, ALTHOUGH WHEN I DO IT IN FRONT OF MY KIDS THEY LAUGH AT ME.

HOW I MET CLAUDIA

FIVE MINUTES INTO MY FIRST DATE AFTER SEPARATING FROM MY WIFE.

WHAT'S YOUR NET WORTH? WHAT ARE THE DETAILS OF YOUR DIVORCE? WHY AREN'T YOU WORKING? WHAT'S YOUR PLAN FOR THE FUTURE?

I HAD MET THE GIRL IN AN ELEVATOR THE NIGHT BEFORE. I PRAYED TO GOD THAT SHE WOULD ENTER THE ELEVATOR WITH ME.

SHE DID. GOD IS GOOD.

I GOT OFF THE ELEVATOR ON HER FLOOR. WE TALKED FOR TEN MINUTES. MY PHONE KEPT RINGING. MY FRIEND ON THE TENTH FLOOR (A WOMAN) WANTED TO KNOW WHERE I WAS SINCE THE DOORMAN HAD ANNOUNCED MY PRESENCE ABOUT FIFTEEN MINUTES EARLIER.

SOMEWHERE BETWEEN THE FIRST AND TENTH FLOOR I GOT LOST IN A MAZE IT WOULD TAKE ME TWO MONTHS TO EXIT.

I DIDN'T THINK YOU WERE GOOD LOOKING LAST NIGHT.

YOU'RE COMPLETELY INSANE. I CAN'T GO OUT WITH YOU.

WELCOME TO NEW YORK DATING POST-MARRIAGE. WE WENT OUT FOR TWO MONTHS BUT SHE BROKE UP WITH ME AT LEAST ONCE A WEEK.

DURING THIS TIME, I LET ONE BUSINESS FAIL AND STARTED ANOTHER BUSINESS THAT WAS DOOMED TO FAIL. I INVESTED IN A FEW OTHER BUSINESSES BUT I HAD NO IDEA THEN WHAT WOULD HAPPEN TO THOSE.

AND STILL I KEPT GETTING BROKEN UP WITH AT LEAST ONCE A WEEK, IF NOT MORE.

I MOVED INTO A TWO BEDROOM APARTMENT SO MY KIDS COULD VISIT ME. BY THE TIME THEY LEFT EACH WEEKEND, THE FLOOR WAS COVERED WITH FOOD, GAMES, BOOKS, VIDEOS, WHATEVER.

THEN I'D SEE MY FRIEND AGAIN ON MONDAYS AND SHE'D BREAK UP WITH ME ON TUESDAYS.

I FINALLY DECIDED TO TAKE IT SERIOUSLY. BACK TO THE DAILY PRACTICE FOR THE FIRST TIME IN THREE YEARS. I WANTED TO MEET SOMEONE I WOULD MARRY. I'M AN UGLY GUY AND HAD NO PROSPECTS AT THAT MOMENT, SO NOT THE EASIEST THING.

NAME:
Claudia Azula

LOCATION:
New York, NY

AGE:

INTERESTS
Yoga, Dance

MUSIC:
Madonna, Points

MOVIES:

JEW
SINGL

So you're from Buenos Aires? I've always wanted to go to Brazil.

That's nice, but Buenos Aires is in Argentina.

You seem really different. Maybe we could meet for dinner?

No dinner. Just tea.

Come on, dinner.

No. Tea!

WE MET FOR TEA EARLY IN THE AFTERNOON ONE DAY. SHE TOLD ME SHE WAS INTO YOGA. WE TALKED FOR A LONG TIME AND IT WAS NICE. WE TOOK A WALK.

Tea HOUSE

WE HAD ALREADY RUN OUT OF TOPICS TO TALK ABOUT. THERE WAS NOTHING BUT SILENCE UNTIL SHE HAD TO GO. BUT I FELT CALM. WE MUST HAVE SAT LIKE THAT IN SILENCE FOR ABOUT FIFTEEN MINUTES. IT'S HARD TO SIT IN SILENCE WITH SOMEONE BUT IT WASN'T HARD THIS TIME.

I HAVE TO CATCH A TRAIN. I'M SELLING MY HOUSE.

WHERE WILL YOU MOVE?

MAYBE THE EAST VILLAGE.

NO, YOU AREN'T. YOU'RE GOING TO MOVE TO THE CORNER OF WALL STREET AND BROAD...

...WHERE I LIVE.

WE'VE BEEN MARRIED NOW FOR OVER A YEAR.

THE WU-TANG CLAN, HITLER, AND SURVIVING YOUR FIRST YEAR OF BEING AN ENTREPRENEUR

THE FIRST DAY I BECAME AN ENTREPRENEUR I CRIED. I HAD ALREADY BEEN RUNNING A COMPANY, RESET, ON THE SIDE WHILE I WORKED AT HBO FULLTIME AND I COULDN'T KEEP CONDUCTING BUSINESS FROM MY CUBICLE. MY BOSS, HIS BOSS, HIS BOSS, HIS BOSS, AND HIS BOSS, WERE ALREADY SUSPICIOUS OF ME.

TWO WEEKS EARLIER...

THE WU-TANG CLAN WANTS US TO DO WEBSITES FOR ALL OF THEIR BACK CD'S AND WE'LL DO WEBSITES FOR EVERY OTHER GROUP THAT LOUD RECORDS HAS.

I RAN THE NUMBERS IN MY HEAD. MAYBE IT WOULD BE $900,000 WORTH OF WORK. THE WU-TANG CLAN WAS INTO CHESS AND BOXING AND THEY WANTED ME SPECIFICALLY TO HELP THEM. THEY HAD AN ALBUM CALLED "THE MYSTERY OF CHESS-BOXING." IT WAS MY FAVORITE ALBUM AT THE TIME BECAUSE WHAT DID I CARE.

FORGET THE WU-TANG CLAN. THEY'RE SCUMBAGS. WHY WOULD YOU WANT TO DO BUSINESS WITH THEM?

HBO

JUST THE OTHER DAY IT WAS A DONE DEAL. I WAS PRACTICALLY IN THE WU-TANG CLAN. THEY "LOVED" ME.

26

SOMETHING HAD GONE HORRIBLY WRONG. IN THE MUSIC BUSINESS, PERSON A PAYS PERSON B WHO PAYS PERSON C, WHO THEN SOMEHOW RETURNS THE FAVOR. BUT IT'S A GAME OF OPERATOR WHERE MONEY IS WHISPERED INTO EVERYONE'S EAR BEFORE BEING PASSED ALONG. BY THE END OF THE TELEPHONE CHAIN, SOMEONE'S OUT OF BUSINESS, EVERYONE'S PAID MONEY, AND EVERYONE IS ANGRY AT EVERYONE ELSE.

THE DEAL WAS OVER.

CRISP

I MADE A FEW MORE CALLS BUT NOBODY WOULD TALK TO ME. I WASN'T AT HBO ANYMORE. I CRIED A BIT WHEN I REALIZED HOW RADICALLY I HAD CHANGED MY LIFE WITHOUT HAVING ANY IDEA OF WHAT I WAS DOING.

THIS WAS IN A WORLD BEFORE VENTURE CAPITALISTS. IF YOU HAD A BUSINESS, YOU NEEDED TO MAKE MONEY. YOU NEEDED TO CALL PEOPLE AND SELL THEM ALL DAY LONG.

AT NIGHT YOU NEEDED TO LAY AWAKE FIGURING OUT HOW YOU WERE GOING TO PAY THE PEOPLE YOU PROMISED THE WORLD TO. BECAUSE BUSINESS IS RELIGION AND YOUR EMPLOYEES ARE YOUR FOLLOWERS.

THERE WERE NO PARTIES, OR "SUMMITS," THEN, FOR FOUNDERS. YOU TRASHED YOUR COMPETITORS TO EVERYONE YOU COULD. NOBODY WAS YOUR FRIEND AND WE ALL WORKED WITHIN A FIVE-BLOCK RADIUS.

HIRE FREELANCERS SO YOU CAN ALWAYS FIRE THEM WHEN THE REVENUES INVARIABLY DIP. YOUR OLD CUSTOMERS ARE YOUR BEST NEW CUSTOMERS. OFFER MORE AND MORE SERVICES TO THEM. IT'S HARD FOR THEM TO SAY NO. SAY "YES" TO EVERYTHING WHEN YOU ARE SELLING. DO ANYTHING TO ADD TO YOUR CLIENT LIST. THE SERVICES BUSINESS FOR A SERVICE THAT NOBODY UNDERSTANDS (WEB DEVELOPMENT BACK THEN) IS ENORMOUSLY PROFITABLE BUT YOU NEED YOUR FOOT IN THE DOOR. THEN YOU FIGURE OUT THE PROFIT. COROLLARY TO ABOVE: MAKE IT AS EASY AS POSSIBLE FOR THEM TO SAY YES. OFFER TO DO STUFF FOR FREE UNTIL THEY SAY YES. DO FAVORS FOR AS MANY PEOPLE AS YOU CAN. YOU CAN'T GIVE BRIBES BUT IF YOU SPEND YOUR ENTIRE LIFE DOING FAVORS FOR CLIENTS THEN EVENTUALLY SOMEONE WILL REPAY THE FAVOR. GIVE CLIENTS ADVICE ON THEIR BUSINESS. FIND PEOPLE JOBS, GIRL-FRIENDS, SEND ENORMOUS GIFT PACKAGES AT CHRISTMAS (OR BIRTHDAYS, VALENTINE'S DAY, OR JUST FOR THE HECK OF IT), DO THINGS FOR THEIR CHARITIES. FIRE ANY EMPLOYEE INSTANTLY WHO HAS A NEGATIVE ATTITUDE. NEGATIVITY IS A CANCER. IT CAN'T BE CURED (BY YOU) AND IT SPREADS QUICKLY THROUGH THE REST OF YOUR COMPANY. ASK CLIENTS FOR ADVICE ABOUT YOUR BUSINESS. MAKE THEM FEEL INVOLVED, ALMOST LIKE OWNERS, WITHOUT GIVING THEM EQUITY. NEW CLIENTS ARE YOUR BEST SALESPEOPLE BECAUSE THEY WANT THEIR PEERS TO HELP THEM FEEL JUSTIFIED IN THEIR DECISIONS. LOOK FOR THE HALF-CHEWED LEFTOVERS FROM YOUR COMPETITORS THAT ARE GROWING FASTER THAN YOU. THEIR OLDER CLIENTS WILL BEGIN TO HATE THEM. NEVER DO A DEAL WHERE SOMEONE ELSE IS RE-SELLING YOUR SERVICES. NOBODY ELSE CARES. FOLLOW UP WITH POTENTIAL CLIENTS BY ASKING THEM TO DINNER OR BREAKFAST. PICK THE NICEST PLACE. PICK UP THE TAB. ASK THEM ABOUT THEIR LOVE LIFE. NEVER LISTEN TO ANYONE WHO SAYS, "I WANT TO MAKE YOU RICH." THEY DON'T. IF SOMEONE STEERS YOU THE WRONG WAY ONCE, NEVER LISTEN TO THEM AGAIN. OVER-PROMISE AND OVER-DELIVER, BUT ONLY THE FIRST TIME. IF SOMEONE SAYS, "I'M TAKING A BIG CHANCE BY HIRING YOU," ASSUME THAT YOU'LL NEVER DO BUSINESS WITH THEM AGAIN AND GET PAID AS QUICKLY AS POSSIBLE. IF A CLIENT SAYS, "I'D RATHER HAVE THIS CONVERSATION IN OUR OFFICES," DON'T GO THERE. NEVER GO THERE AGAIN. IF SOMEONE WANTS TO BUY YOUR COMPANY, IMMEDIATELY LOOK FOR A BETTER OFFER.

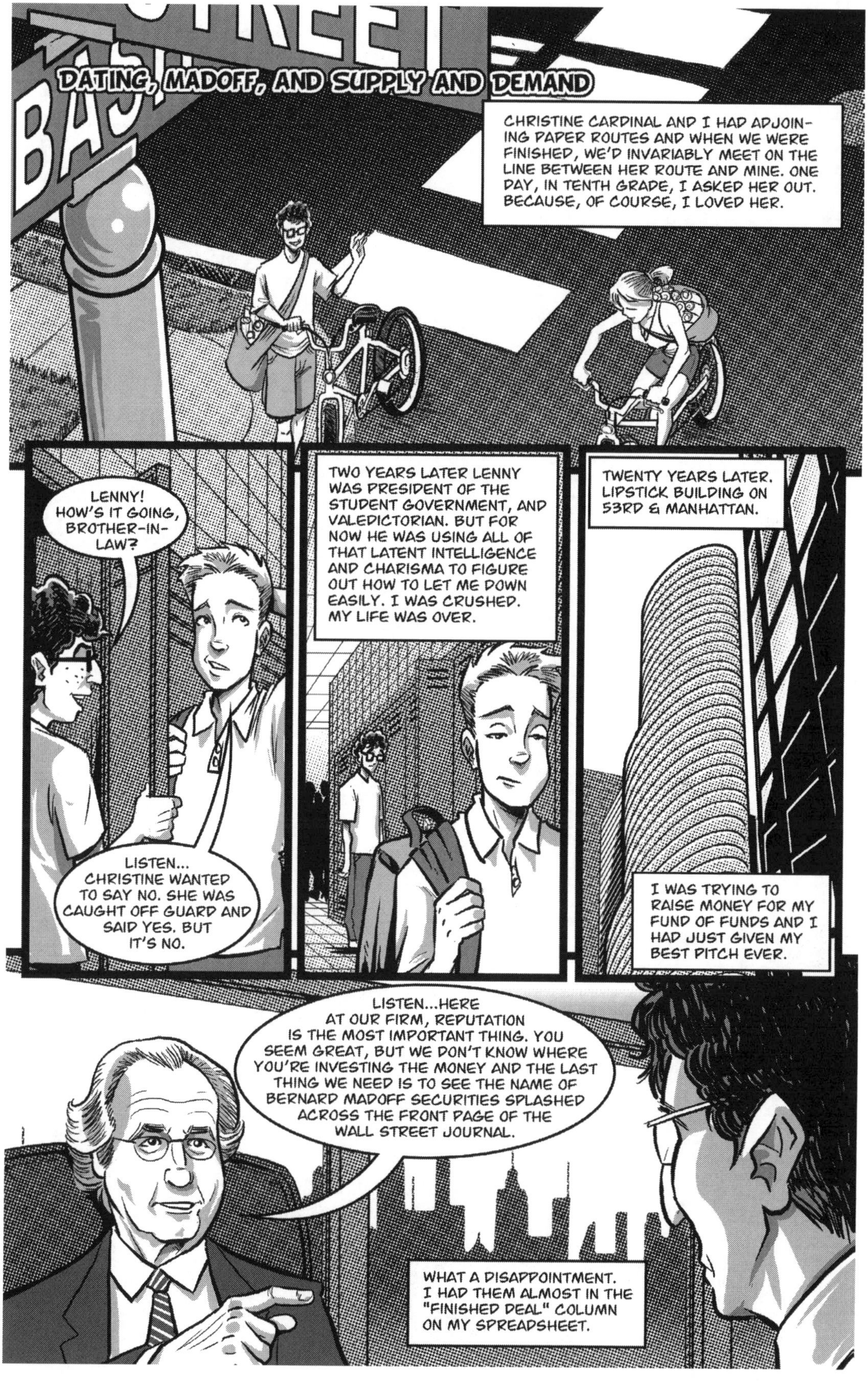
DATING, MADOFF, AND SUPPLY AND DEMAND
CHRISTINE CARDINAL AND I HAD ADJOINING PAPER ROUTES AND WHEN WE WERE FINISHED, WE'D INVARIABLY MEET ON THE LINE BETWEEN HER ROUTE AND MINE. ONE DAY, IN TENTH GRADE, I ASKED HER OUT. BECAUSE, OF COURSE, I LOVED HER.
LENNY! HOW'S IT GOING, BROTHER-IN-LAW?
LISTEN... CHRISTINE WANTED TO SAY NO. SHE WAS CAUGHT OFF GUARD AND SAID YES. BUT IT'S NO.
TWO YEARS LATER LENNY WAS PRESIDENT OF THE STUDENT GOVERNMENT, AND VALEDICTORIAN. BUT FOR NOW HE WAS USING ALL OF THAT LATENT INTELLIGENCE AND CHARISMA TO FIGURE OUT HOW TO LET ME DOWN EASILY. I WAS CRUSHED. MY LIFE WAS OVER.
TWENTY YEARS LATER. LIPSTICK BUILDING ON 53RD & MANHATTAN.
I WAS TRYING TO RAISE MONEY FOR MY FUND OF FUNDS AND I HAD JUST GIVEN MY BEST PITCH EVER.
LISTEN...HERE AT OUR FIRM, REPUTATION IS THE MOST IMPORTANT THING. YOU SEEM GREAT, BUT WE DON'T KNOW WHERE YOU'RE INVESTING THE MONEY AND THE LAST THING WE NEED IS TO SEE THE NAME OF BERNARD MADOFF SECURITIES SPLASHED ACROSS THE FRONT PAGE OF THE WALL STREET JOURNAL.
WHAT A DISAPPOINTMENT. I HAD THEM ALMOST IN THE "FINISHED DEAL" COLUMN ON MY SPREADSHEET.

A FEW MONTHS LATER I WAS IN KEN STARR'S OFFICE. NOT *THAT* KEN STARR. THE OTHER ONE.

I'M RETURNING 20% PER YEAR UP HERE. YOU'RE JUST RETURNING 11%. WHAT DO I NEED YOU FOR?

KENNETH I. STARR

A FEW YEARS LATER BOTH WOULD BE SITTING IN JAIL FOR RUNNING PONZI SCHEMES, BUT FOR NOW I WAS AGAIN CRUSHED AND WONDERING WHAT SORTS OF MESSAGES LIFE WAS SENDING ME.

57867   75391

PEOPLE SAY "NO" FOR MANY DIFFERENT REASONS. FEW OF THOSE REASONS HAVE ANYTHING TO DO WITH YOU.

STREET
BASI

(WELL, CHRISTINE CARDINAL'S "NO" WAS DIRECTLY RELATED TO ME. BUT WHO KNOWS THE EXACT CHEMISTRY GOING THROUGH HER MIND AT THAT TIME.)

EVERYTHING WE GET IN LIFE HAS TO DO WITH SUPPLY AND DEMAND AND HOW OUR PSYCHOLOGY RIDES THAT BALANCE BETWEEN THE TWO. WHEN I WAS HELPING AN INVESTOR OF MINE SELL HIS HEALTHCARE COMPANY, WE HAD TO APPROACH 20 POTENTIAL ACQUIRERS, FOR 5 "SECOND CALLS," TWO ACTUAL MEETINGS, AND ONE FINAL "YES."* BUT THAT MEANS 19 "NO'S" BEFORE GETTING TO THAT ONE YES. THAT WAS THE FUNCTION OF CREATING OUR OWN SUPPLY AND DEMAND.

*AND THEN THREE MONTHS OF HELL, BUT THAT'S ANOTHER STORY.

CREATE THE SUPPLY

ONLINE DATING, FOR BETTER OR WORSE, CREATES SUPPLY IN THE DATING WORLD. YOUR NETWORK OF EVERYONE WHO HAS EVER EMAILED YOU, CREATES SUPPLY FOR ALL SORTS OF OPPORTUNITIES.

GET A QUICK DECISION

WE CALLED THE DECISION MAKER IN EACH COMPANY. WE NEVER STARTED AT THE BOTTOM. YOU CAN'T WASTE TIME ON THE WAY TO YES OR NO.

TRY TO GET AT LEAST ONE YES

AT LEAST SEE OUR PRESENTATION, AT LEAST AGREE TO A SECOND CALL, A MEETING, MEET THE CEO OF THE COMPANY, ETC.

CUT LOSSES QUICKLY

KNOW WHEN TO GIVE UP. CHRISTINE CARDINAL DID NOT WANT TO GO OUT WITH ME. KNOW WHEN TO BACK OFF.

A POTENTIAL CUSTOMER NOW IS A POTENTIAL CUSTOMER LATER. UNLESS YOU ARE PSYCHO. TOO MUCH FOCUS ON ONE POTENTIAL CUSTOMER AND YOU'LL IGNORE THE CROWD THAT MIGHT TRULY BE INTERESTED IN YOUR PRODUCT.

THE MAGIC RATIO

UNDERSTAND THAT THE TYPICAL RATIO IS ABOUT 30:1. YOU NEED TO CONTACT UP TO 30 PEOPLE TO SELL YOUR BUSINESS, OR RAISE INITIAL MONEY FOR YOUR FUND, OR GET A JOB, OR WHATEVER. WHAT THIS ALSO MEANS, IS THAT IF THE SUPPLY IN THE MARKET YOU ARE AIMING FOR IS NOT 30 (I.E. IF YOU ARE BUILDING A PRODUCT THAT ONLY GOOGLE WOULD EVER WANT TO BUY) THEN YOU ARE PROBABLY IN THE WRONG MARKET.

IDEAS

GOOD IDEAS IN YOUR HEAD ARE RULED BY SUPPLY AND DEMAND. YOU NEED TO COME UP WITH 30 IDEAS BEFORE THE RIGHT IDEA COMES ALONG WHICH THERE MIGHT BE DEMAND FOR.

IN 1996, I VISITED A FRIEND OF MINE, ZACH, WHO WORKED AS A PROGRAMMER IN AN ONLINE SEX ... I DON'T KNOW WHAT YOU CALL IT. A STORE? A FACILITY? ALL NIGHT LONG GUYS WOULD PAY FOR THESE GIRLS TO UNDRESS IN THESE CUBICLES AND CHAT WITH THEM OVER THE INTERNET.

VIDEO TECHNOLOGY WASN'T WHAT IT IS TODAY SO IT WAS SORT OF LIKE THE GUYS WOULD GET A BUNCH OF PHOTOS ONE AFTER THE OTHER. IN THE MEANTIME, THE GIRL WOULD IM THEM AND THEY WOULD PAY ABOUT $5 A MINUTE.

PROFILE
NAME
Candy
AGE
18
TURN ONS
Nerdy, Jewish, Hedge Fund Managers

HOW'S THE WORK GOING?

THE GIRLS HERE LOVE ME AND AFTER A LONG NIGHT, IT'S EASY TO 'HANG OUT' WITH THEM.

MY FRIEND'S JOB WAS TO MAKE SURE EVERYTHING KEPT WORKING. THEY WERE GETTING A LOT OF TRAFFIC FOR BACK THEN. THINGS COULD GO DOWN. AND WHEN THINGS WENT DOWN, MONEY WAS LOST. TIME EQUALS MONEY AND TIME EQUALS BRAND. IF YOU'RE UP 24 HOURS A DAY, THEN THE BRAND STAYS FRESH AND MONEY IS MADE. ZACH MADE ABOUT $100K A YEAR BECAUSE NOBODY WAS BETTER THAN HIM AT KEEPING ALL THE WIRES GOING.

NEXT TIME YOU SEE ME I'M GOING TO LOOK COMPLETELY DIFFERENT. I'M GOING TO HAVE LARGER BREASTS! SEE YOU LATER!

I'M AN ADDICT.

IF I DIDN'T LOOK AT FOUR NAKED GIRLS ALL NIGHT LONG, I WOULD FEEL EMPTY INSIDE.

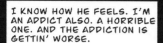

I KNOW HOW HE FEELS. I'M AN ADDICT ALSO. A HORRIBLE ONE. AND THE ADDICTION IS GETTIN' WORSE.

AT FIRST IT WASN'T SO BAD. I'D WRITE A BOOK, WHICH WOULD TAKE ME SIX MONTHS OR SO, AND WHEN THE BOOK CAME OUT I'D LOOK FOR REVIEWS, I'D LOOK FOR PEOPLE TALKING ABOUT IT ON MESSAGE BOARDS, I'D CHECK MY EMAIL ALL NIGHT TO SEE IF PEOPLE WERE WRITING TO ME ABOUT THE BOOK, ETC. BUT AFTER I WROTE THE SECOND BOOK I KNEW I NEEDED MORE.

JUST LIKE ZACH AND THE ALL NIGHT CUSTOMERS OF HIS PLACE OF EMPLOY, I NEED CONSTANT STIMULUS.

I STARTED WRITING MORE ARTICLES. EVEN THOUGH I WAS FULL-TIME RUNNING A FUND OF FUNDS MY MAIN NEEDS WERE MET BY WRITING TWO, MAYBE THREE OR FOUR ARTICLES A DAY FOR THE FINANCIAL TIMES OR THESTREET.COM OR FORBES OR YAHOO, AND HOPING I GET MORE AND MORE FEEDBACK. ANY FEEDBACK, POSITIVE OR NEGATIVE.

NOW TWITTER FEEDS THE ADDICTION. A PITHY THOUGHT IN A FEW SECONDS. 140 CHARACTERS AND WAIT SECONDS FOR SOMEONE TO RESPOND, RETWEET, SHARE IT, FACEBOOK IT, WHATEVER. IF MORE THAN A FEW SECONDS GO BY... DESPAIR.

LAST 3 HOURS

J. Altucher in New Y...
Became the king of online addiction
1 hour ago

Claudia Altucher in N...
Great Yoga workout to...
Yesterday

...nnant

THE CREATIVITY-FEEDBACK LOOP IS NOW ALMOST INSTANTANEOUS. FOURSQUARE IS EVEN BETTER. YOU DON'T EVEN HAVE TO WRITE SOMETHING. YOU JUST HAVE TO BE SOMEWHERE AND PEOPLE CAN RESPOND: MAYBE THEY CAN SHOW UP THERE, OR RT THAT YOU EXIST SOMEWHERE. ACKNOWL-EDGEMENT THAT YOU EXIST AS A PERSON SIMPLY BECAUSE OTHER PEOPLE RECOGNIZE THAT A THOUGHT YOU HAVE, OR A PLACE WHERE YOU HAPPEN TO BE, IS REAL AND SPECIAL BECAUSE IT INVOLVES YOU.

my Face

Businesses that work now (foursquare, Groupon, twitter, penny auction sites like justhaute, zynga, etc.) provide that instant stimulus that the world now craves. I don't know how to get off the train.

But if it's not too much trouble, can you spare a tweet about this comic?

POST   CANCEL

33

WHY I'M AN OPTIMIST

I'M TELLING YOU RIGHT NOW TO PULL THE PLUG ON ME AND LET ME DIE. THERE'S AN IPOD IN MY HEART AND IT JUST NEEDS CHARGING IN ORDER FOR ME TO KEEP GOING, LIVING A MINIMAL EXISTENCE OF NO MOVING, SEMI-BREATHING, BARELY THINKING. DO ME A FAVOR. IF WE GET TO THAT INTIMATE MOMENT WHERE I'M LYING IN THERE AND YOU'RE STANDING OUT THERE, WITH THE DECISION IN YOUR POWER, PULL THE PLUG.

IT'S OVER. UNPLUG HIM.

IN 2003, MY DAD HAD A STROKE.

DOWN THE HALL THERE WAS AN ORTHODOX WOMAN WHO HAD BEEN IN A CAR ACCIDENT WITH HER DAUGHTER. THE WOMAN WAS IN A COMA BUT THE ORTHODOX JEWS COULDN'T UNPLUG HER BECAUSE THAT WAS THEIR RELIGION. IT ONLY TOOK A FEW DAYS ANYWAY AND THE MOTHER'S LIFE DRIBBLED AWAY.

TWO YEARS LATER MY DAD WAS STILL ALIVE, NEVER ONCE HAVING UTTERED A WORD OR MADE A CONCRETE MOTION AFTER HAVING THAT STROKE. HIS EYES WERE OPEN. HE'D BLINK.

SOMETIMES THEY WOULD DROP HIM WHEN MOVING HIM FROM ROOM TO ROOM. OTHER TIMES HE'D GET A BED SORE FROM NOT BEING TURNED AROUND ENOUGH. HIS BED SORES WERE SO BAD THAT HIS SKIN HAD ERODED AWAY TO THE BONE.

34

ONE TIME I TOOK A CHESS POSITION AND BLEW IT UP TO BE THREE FEET BY THREE FEET AND PASTED IT TO THE CEILING SO HE COULD LOOK AT IT SINCE HE WAS LYING ON HIS BACK ALL DAY, UNABLE TO MOVE. BUT THE HOSPITAL HE WAS STAYING AT LOST HIS GLASSES AND HE PROBABLY COULDN'T SEE ANYTHING ANYWAY.

YOU MUST HAVE MIXED FEELINGS. YOU GUYS WERE IN A FIGHT BEFORE HIS STROKE.

TRUE. I HADN'T TALKED TO HIM FOR THE SIX MONTHS BEFORE HIS STROKE. HE SENT ME AN EMAIL ONCE, SAYING I HAD A GOOD TV APPEARANCE. I DIDN'T RESPOND. BUT YOU DON'T GET MIXED FEELINGS AT THOSE POINTS. I WAS PRETTY SURE WHAT MY FEELINGS WERE.

PEOPLE GET ANGRY AT ME SOMETIMES FOR BEING AN OPTIMIST. LOOK AT THE MESSAGE BOARD OF ANY ARTICLE I WRITE. THE LATEST ARTICLE I WROTE HAS OVER 100 COMMENTS (ACROSS TWO DIFFERENT SITES), MOST OF THEM LIKE MINI-HATEMAILS TO ME.

.com

james put down the meth pipe

anonamo
Really you need to be placed upon the firing line.

AWSUMX8!!!!!1!
Ur nothing but a propagandist

Ben10
Stop spewing lies. it makes you look stupid.

POST

I'M NOT AN OPTIMIST AT ALL. WHEN I LOOK AT YOU ALL I SEE IS A STROKE VICTIM WAITING TO HAPPEN. INNOVATIONS IN TECHNOLOGY KEEPING YOU ALIVE AS LONG YOUR FAMILY WANTS YOU TO BE.

DON'T WORRY. HE HAS NO IDEA WHAT'S GOING ON. HIS BRAIN ISN'T THERE.

THE DAY AFTER HE DIED I WROTE TWO ARTICLES FOR THESTREET.COM ABOUT INTERNET STOCKS AND ONE ARTICLE FOR THE FINANCIAL TIMES ABOUT WARREN BUFFETT. I DIDN'T CARE. HE HAD BEEN DEAD FOR TWO YEARS AS FAR AS I WAS CONCERNED.

I DIDN'T EVEN WANT TO GO TO THE FUNERAL, STANDING THERE IN THE MUD AND RAIN WAITING FOR NOTHING TO HAPPEN TO SOMEONE WHO HADN'T BEEN THERE FOR YEARS.

35

HE WAS THE OPTIMIST. CONVINCING ME IN 2002 THAT STOCKS WERE CHEAP RIGHT WHEN I WAS MOST DIS-COURAGED. ENCOURAGING ME IN 1991, IN MY FIRST JOB, TO ASK FOR $90 AN HOUR AS A CONSULTANT. HE WANTED TO BE A SALESMAN FOR MY FIRST COMPANY, CALLING FORTUNE 500 CEOS COLD AND ASKING THEM IF THEY NEEDED WEBSITES.

HE TOLD ME ONCE THAT FOR EVERY CHESS MOVE HE WOULD START LOOKING FIRST AT HOW HE COULD SACRIFICE HIS QUEEN, THE MOST VALUABLE PIECE ON THE BOARD. HE WAS ALWAYS OPTIMISTIC HE COULD START AN ATTACK SOME-WHERE, NEVER REALIZING WHEN HIS ATTACKS WERE LONG SPENT AND HIS POSITION, ONCE SO HAPPY AND GRAND, HAD BEGUN TO SLIP INTO A FRAGILITY THAT CALLED FOR STRIDENT DEFENSE.

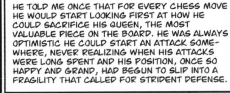

I WAS THE ONE ALWAYS ON THE ROPES, ALWAYS DEFENDING AS HE UNLEASHED ATTACK AFTER ATTACK, NEVER GIVING UP OR SLOWING DOWN, ALWAYS CONVINCED THE WINNING MOVE WAS RIGHT AROUND THE CORNER. ALL I LEARNED WAS DEFENSE.

WHEN I WAS 15, I HAD A PAPER ROUTE. I CAME HOME ONE DAY AND WAS BRAGGING TO HIM, "SOME GUY ACCIDENTALLY TIPPED ME AN EXTRA $5."

AT SOME POINT WE CROSS A LINE, WHERE ONCE WE WERE FRESH AND FIGURING OUT HOW TO CONQUER THE WORLD. THERE COMES A SMALL INSIGNIFICANT MOMENT WHEN YOU HAVE TO DECIDE, "IF IT HAPPENS TO ME, I WOULD WANT THE PLUG TO BE PULLED."

WHEN I WAS 9 AND HE HEARD THAT I CALLED THE THIRD GRADE TEACHER "AN OLD CROW" IT WAS THE FIRST AND ONLY TIME HE EVER HIT ME, HE WAS SO UPSET. WHEN HE INSISTED I LEARN BASIC ECONOMICS HE GAVE ME JUDE WANNISKI'S BOOK, "THE WAY THE WORLD WORKS." BUT WHEN I WAS TEN AND REALLY TRYING TO LEARN HOW THE WORLD WORKS I WOULD SNEAK OFF WITH "CANDY" BY TERRY SOUTHERN OR "BOYS & GIRLS TOGETHER" BY WILLIAM GOLDMAN FROM HIS BOOKSHELF.

HE IMMEDIATELY DROVE ME OVER TO THE GUY'S HOUSE AND MADE ME RETURN THE MONEY.

IT'S A DOTTED LINE IN THE SAND. BUT ONCE YOU CROSS IT YOU CAN'T SAY YOU'RE YOUNG ANYMORE.

HOW TO BE THE LUCKIEST GUY ON THE PLANET IN 4 EASY STEPS

I'M A LUCKY GUY, DAD.

OH YEAH? BUT ARE YOU LUCKY IN LOVE?

EW!

LOVE WAS THE MOST DISGUSTING THING IN THE WORLD TO ME. LOVE WAS LIVING IN ANOTHER NEIGHBORHOOD AT THAT TIME. OR ON ANOTHER PLANET. IT WOULD BE YEARS BEFORE LOVE STUCK ITS UGLY LITTLE NOSE INTO MY HOUSE AND SAID, "HELLO, ANYONE HERE?"

LUCK WAS ALL ABOUT ROLLING THE DICE. OR FINDING A QUARTER ON THE GROUND. OR SEEING A DOUBLE RAINBOW AFTER A QUICK STORM.

BUT NOW I'M DIFFERENT. I'M CONSTANTLY CHECKING IN AND OUT OF THE HOSPITAL OF NO LUCK. I'M OLDER. I NEED LUCK TO BE CONSTANTLY TRANSFUSED INTO ME OR I RUN OUT OF IT. FOR ME, GOOD LUCK EQUALS HAPPINESS.

1. BE HAPPY.
2. ERADICATE UNHAPPINESS.
3. EVERY DAY SHOULD BE AS SMOOTH AS POSSIBLE. NO HASSLES.

I GET LUCKY WHEN I STICK TO THREE SIMPLE GOALS.

THERE'S BEEN AT LEAST TEN TIMES IN MY LIFE THAT EVERYTHING SEEMED SO LOW I FELT LIKE I WOULD NEVER ACHIEVE THE ABOVE THREE THINGS AND THE WORLD WOULD BE BETTER OFF WITHOUT ME. OTHER TIMES I FELT LIKE I WAS STUCK AT A CROSSROADS AND WOULD NEVER FIGURE OUT WHICH ROAD TO TAKE. EACH TIME I BOUNCED BACK.

1. BE HAPPY
2. ERADICATE UNHAPPINESS.
3. EVERY DAY SHOULD BE AS SMOOTH AS POSSIBLE. NO HASSLES.

PHYSICAL
EMOTIONAL
MENTAL
SPIRITUAL

WHEN I LOOK BACK AT THESE TIMES NOW I REALIZE THERE WAS A COMMON THREAD. EACH TIME THERE WERE FOUR THINGS, AND ONLY FOUR THINGS, THAT WERE ALWAYS IN PLACE IN ORDER FOR ME TO BOUNCE BACK. NOW I TRY TO INCORPORATE THESE FOUR THINGS INTO A DAILY PRACTICE SO I NEVER DIP LOW AGAIN.

THE DAILY PRACTICE

PHYSICAL

BEING IN SHAPE. DOING SOME FORM OF EXERCISE. YOU CAN'T BE HAPPY IF YOU AREN'T HEALTHY. ALSO, SPENDING THIS TIME HELPS YOUR MIND BETTER DEAL WITH ITS DAILY ANXIETIES. IF YOU CAN BREATHE EASY WHEN YOUR BODY IS IN PAIN THEN IT'S EASIER TO BREATHE DURING DIFFICULT SITUATIONS.

EMOTIONAL

IF SOMEONE IS A DRAG ON ME, I CUT THEM OUT. IF SOMEONE LIFTS ME UP, I BRING THEM CLOSER. WHEN THE PLANE IS GOING DOWN, PUT THE OXYGEN MASK ON YOUR FACE FIRST. FAMILY, FRIENDS, PEOPLE I LOVE – I ALWAYS TRY TO BE THERE FOR THEM AND HELP. BUT I DON'T GET CLOSE TO ANYONE BRINGING ME DOWN.

MENTAL

EVERY DAY I WRITE DOWN IDEAS. NO IDEAS TODAY? MEMORIZE ALL THE LEGAL 2-LETTER WORDS FOR SCRABBLE. TRANSLATE THE TAO TE CHING INTO SPANISH.

100 Alternatives to College

THE "IDEA MUSCLE" ATROPHIES WITHIN DAYS IF YOU DON'T USE IT. IT TAKES ABOUT 3-6 MONTHS TO BUILD UP ONCE IT ATROPHIES. TRUST ME ON THIS.

SPIRITUAL

I FEEL THAT MOST PEOPLE DON'T LIKE THE WORD **SPIRITUAL**. THEY THINK IT MEANS "GOD" OR "RELIGION." I DON'T KNOW WHAT IT MEANS. BUT I FEEL LIKE I HAVE A SPIRITUAL PRACTICE WHEN I DO ONE OF THE FOLLOWING: PRAY*, MEDITATE, BE GRATEFUL, PRACTICE FORGIVENESS, STUDY SPIRITUAL TEXT.

*DOESN'T MATTER IF I'M PRAYING TO A GOD OR TO DEAD PEOPLE OR TO THE SUN OR TO A CHAIR IN FRONT OF ME – IT JUST MEANS BEING THANKFUL. AND NOT TAKING ALL THE CREDIT, FOR JUST A FEW SECONDS OF THE DAY.

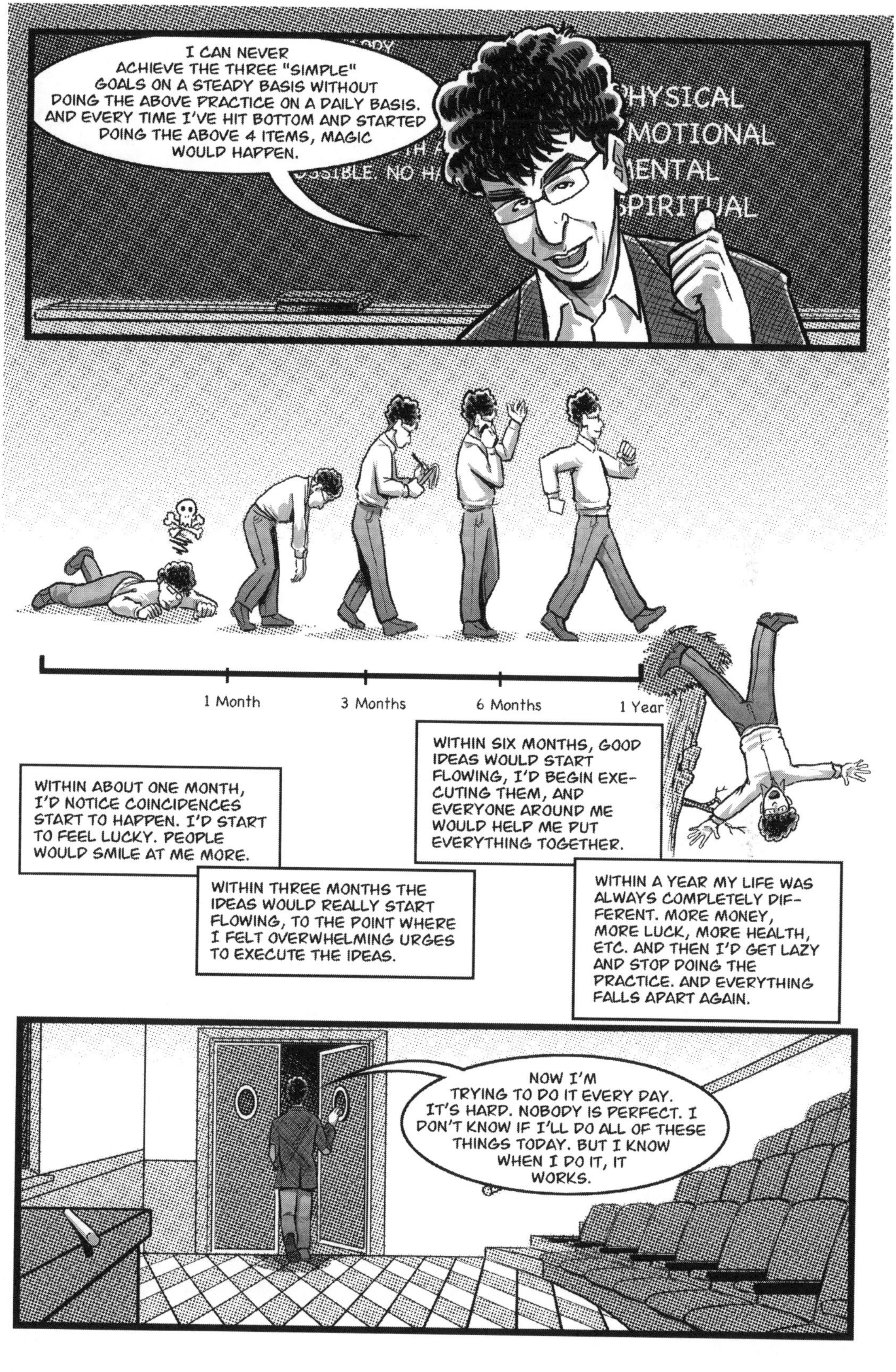
I CAN NEVER ACHIEVE THE THREE "SIMPLE" GOALS ON A STEADY BASIS WITHOUT DOING THE ABOVE PRACTICE ON A DAILY BASIS. AND EVERY TIME I'VE HIT BOTTOM AND STARTED DOING THE ABOVE 4 ITEMS, MAGIC WOULD HAPPEN.
1 Month
3 Months
6 Months
1 Year
WITHIN ABOUT ONE MONTH, I'D NOTICE COINCIDENCES START TO HAPPEN. I'D START TO FEEL LUCKY. PEOPLE WOULD SMILE AT ME MORE.
WITHIN THREE MONTHS THE IDEAS WOULD REALLY START FLOWING, TO THE POINT WHERE I FELT OVERWHELMING URGES TO EXECUTE THE IDEAS.
WITHIN SIX MONTHS, GOOD IDEAS WOULD START FLOWING, I'D BEGIN EXE-CUTING THEM, AND EVERYONE AROUND ME WOULD HELP ME PUT EVERYTHING TOGETHER.
WITHIN A YEAR MY LIFE WAS ALWAYS COMPLETELY DIF-FERENT. MORE MONEY, MORE LUCK, MORE HEALTH, ETC. AND THEN I'D GET LAZY AND STOP DOING THE PRACTICE. AND EVERYTHING FALLS APART AGAIN.
NOW I'M TRYING TO DO IT EVERY DAY. IT'S HARD. NOBODY IS PERFECT. I DON'T KNOW IF I'LL DO ALL OF THESE THINGS TODAY. BUT I KNOW WHEN I DO IT, IT WORKS.

THE WORST VENTURE CAPITAL DECISION IN HISTORY

I MADE THE WORST DECISION IN VENTURE CAPITAL HISTORY IN LATE 2000. I WAS A PARTNER AT A VENTURE FIRM CALLED 212. I HAD A FEW PARTNERS BUT I WON'T SOIL THEIR NAMES WITH THIS STORY. WHAT FOLLOWS WAS COMPLETELY MY FAULT.

DAN, WHAT'S UP?

A FRIEND OF MINE IS VP OF BIZ DEV AT THIS SEARCH ENGINE COMPANY. WE CAN PROBABLY GET 20% OF THE COMPANY FOR $1 MILLION. HE SOUNDS DESPERATE.

WAIT. WHAT?

THEY HELP SEARCH ENGINES FIND PAGES WITH SYNONYMS ON WHAT YOU SEARCH, I THINK.

IT'S PRETTY HARD TO DEFEND HUMANITY, MANAGE $115 MILLION, AND LISTEN TO A PITCH ABOUT A COMPANY CALLED OINGO AT THE SAME TIME.

SEARCH ENGINES? AREN'T THEY ALL DEAD? WHAT'S THE STOCK PRICE ON EXCITE THESE DAYS? YOU KNOW WHAT IT IS? ZERO! NO THANKS.

I WAS VERY QUICK WITH MY DECISIONS BACK THEN.

EXCITE WAS IN THE PROCESS OF GOING BANKRUPT. LYCOS WAS QUICKLY DISAPPEARING. YAHOO'S STOCK WAS IN THE GUTTER. AND NOW THIS WAS A RANDOM SEARCH ENGINE SOFTWARE COMPANY THAT WAS PROBABLY GOING TO GO BANKRUPT.

WELL, OINGO SOMEHOW MANAGED TO RAISE SOME MONEY AND STAY AFLOAT. IN 2003, A LITTLE SEARCH ENGINE COMPANY CALLED GOOGLE BOUGHT THEM. GOOGLE NEEDED THE OINGO SOFTWARE IN ORDER TO GENERATE 99% OF ITS REVENUES AT IPO TIME. GOOGLE PAID 1% OF THE COMPANY IN STOCK, A STAKE THAT WOULD NOW BE WORTH $1.5BB. SO OUR ONE MILLION DOLLAR INVESTMENT COULD'VE BEEN WORTH ABOUT $300 MILLION, GIVE OR TAKE.

GAME OVER

SOMETIMES I'M NOT VERY BRIGHT.

SHORTLY AFTER I MADE THE DECISION NOT TO INVEST IN OINGO, INVESTCORP DECIDED TO ABSORB 212 VENTURES AND BUY OUT OUR CONTRACTS. THEY OFFERED ME A CHANCE TO STAY THERE AS AN EMPLOYEE, BUT I'M NOT A VERY GOOD EMPLOYEE. AS FOR THE "DEFENDER" GAME IN MY OFFICE, ONE OF MY PARTNERS AT 212 VENTURES HAD A BAD GAME.

HAVE A NICE LIFE.

I NEVER SPOKE TO HIM AGAIN. WHICH IS A SHAME, BECAUSE HE WAS THE BEST NEGOTIATOR I EVER KNEW.

I'VE MADE A LOT WORSE DECISIONS IN LIFE THAN NOT INVESTING IN OINGO. WITHIN TWO YEARS OF THE OINGO DECISION I WAS CLOSE TO BROKE AND HAD TO SELL MY BEAUTIFUL APARTMENT. THAT WAS WORSE FOR ME. I'M SURE WHAT'S HAPPENED TO ME SINCE THEN WOULD'VE BEEN A LOT LESS INTERESTING IF I HAD INVESTED IN OINGO. WHO KNOWS WHAT WOULD'VE BEEN DIFFERENT? BUT MAYBE I'M JUST TELLING MYSELF THESE THINGS SO I CAN FEEL GOOD. I OFTEN DO THAT.

Office Stuff

More Office Stuff

WHY I WRITE BOOKS EVEN THOUGH I'VE LOST MONEY ON EVERY BOOK I'VE WRITTEN

FOR 12 MONTHS IN A ROW, WITH THE MARKET GOING STRAIGHT DOWN I USED SIGNALS GENERATED BY THE SOFTWARE I HAD WRITTEN IN LATE 2001 TO BUY STOCKS AND I MADE MY MONTHLY NUT. ON DAYS WHEN I LOST MONEY I WOULD CRY.

I HAD TWO KIDS, A HOUSE THAT I COULDN'T SELL, I WAS ALMOST BROKE, AND MY MONTHLY BURN WAS $40,000. I WOULDN'T BE ABLE TO AFFORD DIAPERS AND FOOD FOR MY 2-MONTH-OLD BABY. TWO YEARS EARLIER, TO THE DAY, I LOOKED AT MY BANK STATEMENT AND HAD ABOUT $15,000,000. NOW, LATE 2001, ALMOST NOTHING. I WROTE SOME SOFTWARE TO TRADE WITH WHAT LITTLE MONEY I HAD LEFT.

I HAD A LIFE INSURANCE POLICY SO I FIGURED I COULD KILL MYSELF IN THE WORST CASE AND MY FAMILY COULD LIVE ON THE FOUR MILLION THAT WOULD RESULT. BUT I WAS GOOD, OR LUCKY, OR MY SOFTWARE WAS GOOD, OR GOD WAS WATCHING OUT FOR ME, OR SOME COMBINATION OF THE ABOVE. FOR 12 MONTHS I EKED OUT MY $40,000 A MONTH FROM TRADING AND THEN SOLD MY OVER-INDULGENT LOFT, BECAME A LIVING EXILE FOR A FEW YEARS AND WORKED ON A RECOVERY.

SO I WROTE A BOOK. I WAS TRADING MY SOFTWARE FOR ABOUT FIVE DIFFERENT HEDGE FUNDS OR INDIVIDUALS (FOR EXAMPLE, VICTOR NIEDERHOFFER) AT THAT TIME. PAMELA VAN GIESSEN FROM WILEY, WHO HAD PUBLISHED VICTOR NIEDERHOFFER'S BOOK, WAS THE EDITOR.

I WANT TO WRITE ABOUT THINGS THAT PEOPLE SHOULD AVOID IN THE MARKET.

NO. PEOPLE WANT POSITIVE STUFF. WRITE ABOUT YOUR TECHNIQUES THAT WORK. CALL IT "TRADE LIKE A HEDGE FUND."

SO I DID.

WHEN THE BOOK CAME OUT, NIEDERHOFFER HATED IT. I WAS UP OVER 100% FOR HIM IN THE PRIOR YEAR. HE THOUGHT I WAS GIVING AWAY ALL HIS TECHNIQUES EVEN THOUGH HE ONLY TRADED FUTURES AND MY SIGNALS IN THE BOOK WERE FOR STOCKS AND WERE SIGNALS I HAD BEEN TRADING LONG BEFORE I MET HIM.

I FELT HORRIBLE BECAUSE I LOOKED UP TO HIM SO MUCH. HE TRASHED ME AND THE BOOK ON HIS EMAIL LIST. PEOPLE WHO HAD BEEN MY FRIENDS STOPPED TALKING TO ME ON BLIND FAITH.

YOU ARE A TOTAL LAUGHING STOCK. —NIEDERHOFFER

THE BOOK BECAME CONTROVERSIAL AND BECAME MY BEST SELLING BOOK.

"One of the best books of the year."
-*Barron's*

THE book of the year for 2004.
-*The Stock Trader's Almanac*

I CALLED PAMELA THE OTHER DAY. "HOW MANY BOOKS DID THAT ONE SELL?" 14,074 COPIES. THAT'S IT. AND THAT WAS A BEST SELLER (FOR FINANCE BOOKS). I PROBABLY PULLED ABOUT $25,000 TOTAL FROM IT. SO NOTHING.

PAMELA AND I DECIDED TO WORK ON MY NEXT BOOK.

I WANT TO DO SOMETHING ON WARREN BUFFETT. HOW HE'S A MORE ACTIVE TRADER THAN ANYONE BELIEVES.

GOT IT! DO "TRADE LIKE WARREN BUFFET."

SO I DID. MY ADVANCE: $7,500.

WHY DID I AGREE TO WRITE THIS? I AM NEVER GOING TO WRITE A BOOK AGAIN.

A BOOK IS BRUTAL. IT'S THE WORST THING. YOU DO NOTHING FOR 3-6 MONTHS WHILE YOU WRITE IT. THE BOOK CAME OUT. COMPLETE FAILURE. IN TOTAL 6,552 COPIES WERE SOLD.

I THOUGHT THE RELIGION OF BUFFETT WOULD'VE KICKED IN AT SOME POINT AND HIS FOL-LOWERS WOULD'VE BOUGHT THE BOOK. BUT THE RELIGION HAS HIM AS THE PROPHET OF VALUE INVESTING AND I WAS SAYING HE WASN'T. BLASPHEMY!

SO I DID ANOTHER BOOK. I NEEDED TO RECLAIM THE POSITIVE FEELINGS I FELT WHEN MY FIRST BOOK SOLD OVER 10,000 COPIES. I LOVED THE BOOK "SUPERMONEY" BY ADAM SMITH, WRITTEN IN THE EARLY 70'S. POP FINANCE AT ITS BEST. SO I WROTE 'SUPERCASH' ABOUT HEDGE FUND STRATEGIES. THIS TIME, TO PAMELA'S SURPRISE, I GOT AN AGENT. MY ADVANCE: $30,000.

THE BOOK IS HORRIBLE. I CAN'T EVEN OPEN IT. IT SOLD 1,565 COPIES.

THEN THE STOCK MARKET WENT ON FIRE. AND WITH STOCKPICKR, A SITE MY BUSINESS PARTNER, DAN, AND I BUILT IN LATE 2006 (AND SOLD TO THESTREET.COM IN 2007), I HAD A BUILT-IN AUDIENCE OF A MILLION PEOPLE. I DECIDED TO DO ANOTHER BOOK. PAM COULDN'T BUY IT. I WAS A FAILURE NOW AT WILEY SO THEY PASSED. PENGUIN PICKED IT UP. I FORGET THE EXACT ADVANCE NOW BUT IT WAS SOMEWHERE BETWEEN $80,000-$100,000.

IF I EVER TOLD YOU IT WAS MORE THAN THAT, I PROBABLY LIED ON PURPOSE.

THE BOOK WAS SET FOR PUBLICATION IN DECEMBER 2008. I BEGGED THEM TO WAIT. NOBODY WAS GOING TO BUY A BOOK ABOUT STOCKS CALLED "THE FOREVER PORTFOLIO" IN THE WORST BEAR MARKET IN HISTORY. NOBODY.

PLEASE, PLEASE, **PLEASE**...

I'M SORRY, JAMES. IT'S ON THE SCHEDULE. IT HAS TO GO OUT.

IT SOLD 1,598 COPIES. PEOPLE WERE WORRIED WHETHER OR NOT THEY WERE GOING TO SURVIVE. NOT WHAT STOCKS THEY SHOULD BUY FOR "FOREVER."

You are the smartest person in the world for buying this book

I WENT AROUND TO EVERY BOOKSTORE IN THE CITY. I WOULD WRITE NOTES ON THE INSIDE OF EVERY BOOK AND THEN PUT THEM BACK ON THE BOOKSHELF.

I WANTED TO WRITE ANOTHER BOOK, EVEN THOUGH I'VE HATED THE PROCESS OF WRITING EVERY SINGLE BOOK I'VE EVER WRITTEN. MY AGENT CALLED PENGUIN. THEY DIDN'T WANT IT. I ACTUALLY THINK THEY PERSONALLY HATED ME. I TOLD MY AGENT WHO I WANTED TO DO THE BOOK WITH. IN FACT, THE EXACT EDITOR I WANTED TO DO THE BOOK WITH.

HOLLIS HEIMBOUCH AT HARPER COLLINS.

SHE SENT THE 60-PAGE BOOK PROPOSAL TO 20 EDITORS INCLUDING HOLLIS. I WAS WRITING FOR THE WALL STREET JOURNAL THEN, DOING OTHER STUFF FOR NEWS CORP, AND I THOUGHT IT WOULD BE A PERFECT FIT FOR HER GIVEN THE BOOKS I SAW THAT SHE HAD EDITED. OTHER WRITERS HAD TOLD ME SHE WAS GREAT TO WORK WITH. I HAD DONE MY RESEARCH.

SHE REJECTED IT. ALL 20 EDITORS SHE SENT TO REJECTED THE BOOK.

44

THIS IS A MISTAKE. THIS BOOK IS PERFECT FOR HER. CALL HER AND TAKE HER OUT TO LUNCH.

FIND OUT WHY SHE REJECTED IT. EXPLAIN WHY IT WOULD BE A GOOD BOOK WITH HARPER COLLINS.

YOU NEED TO WINE AND DINE PEOPLE. FIND OUT WHY THEY ARE REJECTING THE BOOK.

SALES IS INFORMATION, IT'S FRIENDSHIPS, IT'S RELATIONSHIPS.

IF YOU'RE GOING TO TELL ME HOW TO DO MY JOB, THIS RELATIONSHIP IS OVER.

...SORRY...

SO I WROTE AN EMAIL TO HOLLIS AND EXPLAINED WHY THE BOOK WOULD BE GOOD FOR HER. SHE AGREED TO MEET ME.

IT'S ABOUT HOW THE MEDIA TRIES TO SCARE THE PUBLIC EVERY WEEK WITH A NEW HORROR STORY: PANDEMICS, GLOBAL WARMING, NUCLEAR TERRORISM, RIOTS IN EGYPT. THE BOOK IS ABOUT EVERY WAY THE WORLD COULD END, AND HOW TO MAKE AS MUCH MONEY AS POSSIBLE OFF OF THESE IMPENDING APOCALYPSES.

THIS PROPOSAL SEEMS LIKE IT WAS WRITTEN BY WIKIPEDIA. YOU NEED TO GIVE US A REAL METHODOLOGY FOR WHAT TO DO WHEN THE END OF THE WORLD HITS. THE IDEAS ARE GREAT; I JUST DON'T LIKE THE WRITING.

THE WSJ STEPPED IN. ROE D'ANGELO WHO RUNS THEIR BOOKS DEPARTMENT THOUGHT IT WAS A GREAT IDEA FOR A BOOK SO THEY BOUGHT IT, HOLLIS AND HARPER AGREED TO EDIT IT, BUT ROE FOUND AN EXCELLENT CO-AUTHOR, DOUG SEASE. HE WOULD WRITE THE INTROS TO EACH CHAPTER. I WOULD WRITE THE IDEAS, ETC., AND HE WOULD SEW IT ALL UP.

Time Spent and Copies Sold

I'VE MADE NO MONEY EVER FROM BOOKS (IF YOU FACTOR IN TIME SPENT ON THEM) AND NOW I'VE WRITTEN FIVE. I MADE MONEY TRADING. AND FROM STOCKPICKR.COM, FROM ANGEL INVESTING, FROM MY FIRST BUSINESS IN THE 90'S, AND FROM THE OCCA- SIONAL DEAL. BUT NET-NET I'VE LOST MONEY AND TIME FROM BOOKS.

IN MAY, 2009, I HAD JUST STARTED DATING SOMEONE. IT WAS OUR FOURTH DATE AND SHE WAS GOING TO MEET ME AT THE PENN STATION BOOKSTORE.

Business Books

SHE LOOKED AROUND AND THOUGHT MAYBE I HAD PLANTED IT THERE SOMEHOW AND WAS SECRETLY WATCHING HER. BUT I WAS LATE TO MEET HER THAT DAY. SHE LOOKED AT THE INSCRIPTION AGAIN.

I ♥ YOU
James Altucher

A LITTLE OVER A YEAR LATER WE GOT MARRIED. AND THAT'S WHY I WRITE BOOKS.

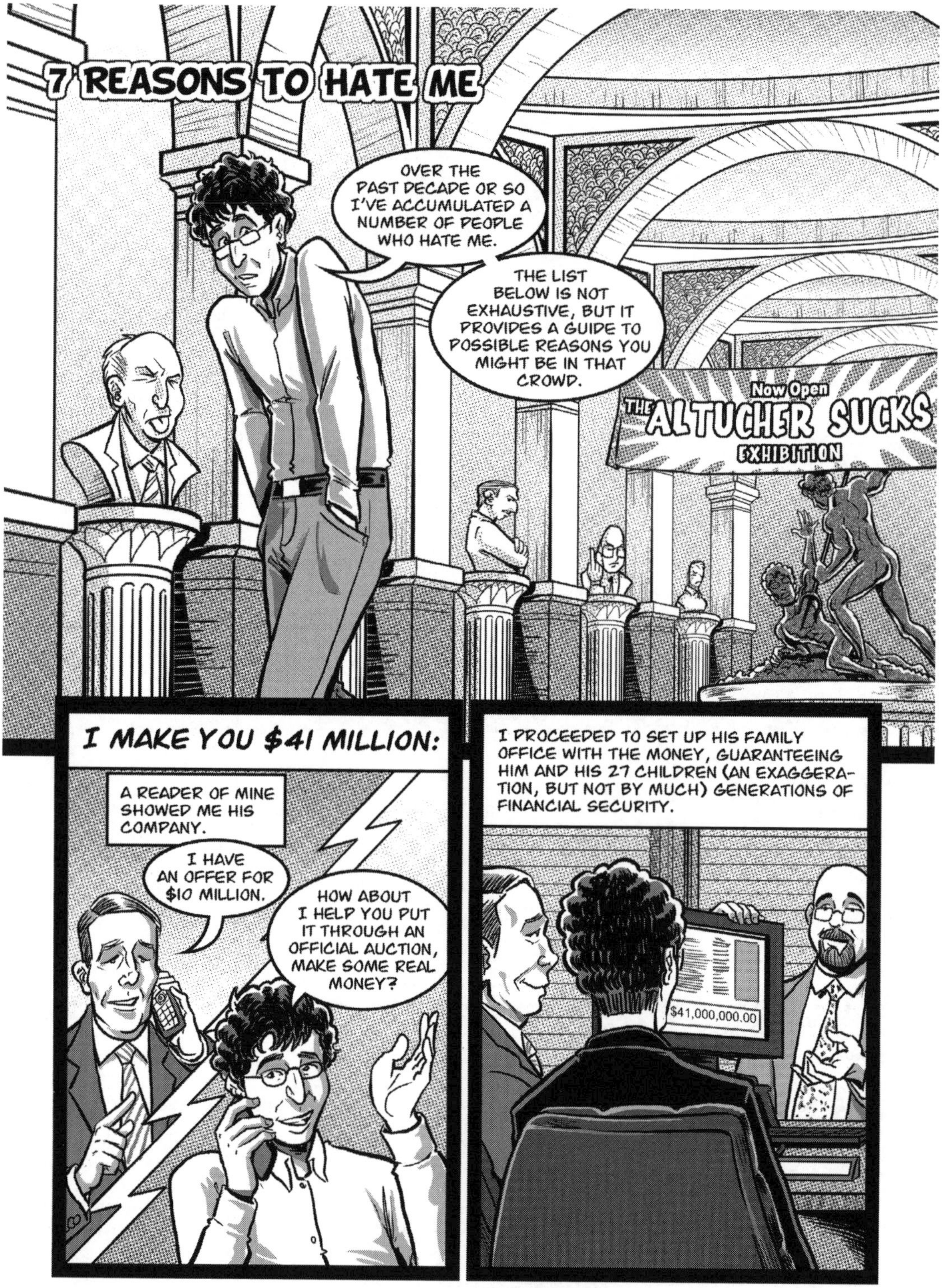
7 REASONS TO HATE ME
OVER THE PAST DECADE OR SO I'VE ACCUMULATED A NUMBER OF PEOPLE WHO HATE ME.
THE LIST BELOW IS NOT EXHAUSTIVE, BUT IT PROVIDES A GUIDE TO POSSIBLE REASONS YOU MIGHT BE IN THAT CROWD.
Now Open THE ALTUCHER SUCKS EXHIBITION
I MAKE YOU $41 MILLION:
A READER OF MINE SHOWED ME HIS COMPANY.
I HAVE AN OFFER FOR $10 MILLION.
HOW ABOUT I HELP YOU PUT IT THROUGH AN OFFICIAL AUCTION, MAKE SOME REAL MONEY?
I PROCEEDED TO SET UP HIS FAMILY OFFICE WITH THE MONEY, GUARANTEEING HIM AND HIS 27 CHILDREN (AN EXAGGERATION, BUT NOT BY MUCH) GENERATIONS OF FINANCIAL SECURITY.
$41,000,000.00

I THEN WENT AND SET UP MY OWN FUND OF FUNDS AND THAT UPSET HIM ENOUGH THAT HE NO LONGER TALKS TO ME. THERE'S MORE TO THE STORY, BUT SUFFICE TO SAY I MADE HIM $41 MILLION AND NOW HE DOESN'T SPEAK TO ME.

I MAKE YOU $3 MILLION.

ANOTHER FRIEND WAS AN INVESTOR IN AN INTERNET COMPANY IN 1999. I INTRODUCED HIM TO A PUBLIC COMPANY THAT WAS DOING A ROLL-UP.

CONSIDERING THAT $3 MILLION I JUST MADE YOU, HOW ABOUT A FINDER'S FEE?

HA! WELCOME TO THE REAL WORLD.

I WRITE A BOOK (OH, AND I MAKE YOU MONEY).

YOU'RE FIRED.

HE DIDN'T LIKE MY BOOK. HE THEN WROTE ON HIS MESSAGE BOARD THAT I HAD COST HIM MONEY. HE HAD TO RECANT WHEN MY ASSOCIATE TOLD HIM WE HAVE COPIES OF THE CHECKS HE PAID US FOR OUR PERFORMANCE FEES.

I RECOMMEND A STOCK THAT YOU LOSE MONEY ON.

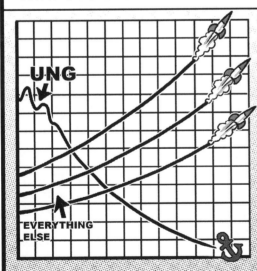

UNG

EVERYTHING ELSE

THIS HAPPENS, ALBEIT RARELY. ABOUT A YEAR AND A HALF AGO, FOR INSTANCE, I RECOMMENDED THE NATURAL GAS ETF, UNG. IT HAS GONE DOWN PRETTY DISASTROUSLY SINCE THEN. DOZENS OF OTHER STOCKS HAVE DONE WELL SINCE I WROTE ABOUT THEM.

BUT IT'S FAIR TO HATE ME FOR YOUR MONEY LOSS. AFTER ALL, I PROBABLY MAKE MOST OF YOUR FINANCIAL DECISIONS FOR YOU AND MAYBE EVEN SOME OF YOUR RELATIONSHIP AND FAMILY DECISIONS.

HONEY, WHAT SHOULD WE WATCH? LOST? 24?

I DON'T KNOW. WHICH ONE DOES ALTUCHER WATCH?

I RECOMMEND A STOCK BE SOLD OR SHORTED.

WHEN I RECOMMENDED A SHORT ON FSLR THERE WERE THESE COMMENTS IN THE MESSAGE BOARDS:

WHAT AN IDIOT **AND** YELLOW JOURNALIST.

I LOOK FORWARD TO POINTING OUT IN THE FUTURE JUST HOW WRONG YOU WERE ABOUT SOLAR IN GENERAL AND FSLR IN PARTICULAR.

WHO'S PAYING YOU THIS TIME?

AGAIN, I TOTALLY UNDERSTAND. IF I WERE LONG A STOCK, AND SOMEONE WAS RECOMMENDING SELLING, I MIGHT ALSO HATE THEM. I MIGHT ACCUSE THEM OF ILLEGAL ACTIVITY OR SCREAM PERSONAL NAMES AT THEM.

WHY NOT? I HAVE NOTHING BETTER TO DO WITH MY DAY THAN SHOUT LOUDLY ON A MESSAGE BOARD.

I'M UGLY.

I PROBABLY SHOULD NEVER GO ON VIDEOS OR TV AGAIN BUT MY KIDS LIKE SEEING ME ON THEM AND SO I TRY TO GO ON AS MUCH AS POSSIBLE.

YAHOO! MESSAGE BOARD

○ MIKE90X

There was some homeless looking guy named James Altucher recommending stocks on CNBC today. Pretty cool of CNBC.

LESSONS I'VE LEARNED FROM THE PEOPLE WHO HATE ME

1.) IF YOU MAKE PEOPLE MONEY, MAKE SURE YOU GET A HUGE FEE. THIS WAY IT DOESN'T MATTER IF THEY HATE YOU AFTERWARD SINCE MONEY BUYS HAPPINESS.

2.) IF YOU RECOMMEND A STOCK, TRY TO MAKE SURE IT GOES UP IMMEDIATELY. YOU HAVE ABOUT 24 HOURS, OR ELSE PEOPLE START HATING YOU.

3.) IF YOU RECOMMEND SHORTING A STOCK, MAKE SURE YOU SAY LOUD AND CLEAR THAT NO HEDGE FUNDS ARE PAYING YOU AND THAT YOU, PERSONALLY, ARE NOT SHORT THE STOCK. THEY STILL WON'T BELIEVE YOU BUT AT LEAST YOU SAID IT UP FRONT.

4.) TRY NOT TO BE UGLY IF YOU GO ON TV. OR ELSE MAYBE WEAR A MASK. IT'S OK IF YOU ARE UGLY IF YOU FOLLOW RULE NO. 2 ABOVE. OR, AS WARREN BUFFETT ONCE SAID--

THE BEST WAY TO BE LOVED IS TO BE LOVABLE.

THE CHELSEA HOTEL, CHUBB ROCK, AND YOU CAN NEVER GO HOME AGAIN.

IT WAS THREE IN THE MORNING AND THE GIRL WAS CRYING ON THE STAIRCASE BETWEEN THE 7TH AND 6TH FLOOR OF THE CHELSEA HOTEL ON 23RD STREET. I LIVED ON THE 9TH FLOOR.

I WALKED PAST THE GIRL AND I DESPERATELY WANTED TO TALK TO HER. I WAS GOING TO BE HER HERO.

ON ANOTHER OCCASION, I TOOK THE ELEVATOR DOWN.

HEY, HOLD THE DOOR!

THANKS, MAN.

SO... WHAT'S THE FREAKIEST THING YOU'VE SEEN ON OUR FLOOR HERE?

THERE WAS THIS GIRL WHO WAS A FEW MONTHS LATE ON HER RENT...

"STANLEY BARD, THE OWNER OF THE HOTEL, CALLED HER AND ASKED HER WHERE THE RENT WAS."

IT'S OKAY. I'M COMING RIGHT DOWN.

AND THEN SHE TOOK A RUNNING LEAP OUT THE WINDOW AND ENDED UP ALL OVER 23RD ST.

COME TO THINK OF IT, THAT WAS IN YOUR ROOM RIGHT BEFORE YOU MOVED IN.

BUT FIRST, THE GIRL WHO WAS CRYING FROM 12 YEARS EARLIER. I REALLY WANTED TO TALK TO HER. ANYTHING COULD HAPPEN. HOW COULD BEAUTIFUL PEOPLE BE SO SAD? AGONY! WHY COULDN'T I TALK TO A CRYING GIRL AT THREE IN THE MORNING?

AGONY LIKE THIS IS ONLY RESERVED FOR THE THINGS WE'RE TOO AFRAID TO DO.

TIMOR, WHO WORKED AT THE FRONT DOOR, TOLD ME A FEW WEEKS LATER THAT THE CRYING GIRL HAD ONCE MADE A MOVIE WHERE SHE WAS TIED UP AND WEARING A MASK THAT BARELY LET HER BREATHE WHILE ANOTHER GIRL DRIPPED HOT WAX ONTO HER VAGINA FOR TWO STRAIGHT HOURS.

YOU MISSED THE PARTY. IT WAS AT THAT CLUB, YOU KNOW THE ONE. THEY SHOWED THE MOVIE ON THE WALL FOR TWO HOURS AND WE ALL HAD TO BUY TWO DRINKS BEFORE WE LEFT.

12 YEARS LATER I WAS LIVING IN THE CHELSEA HOTEL AGAIN, AFTER SEPA-RATING FROM MY WIFE. I THOUGHT FOR A SECOND THAT EVERYTHING WOULD BE OK IF I JUST MOVED BACK TO WHERE I LIVED BEFORE I HAD BEEN MARRIED.

MOLLIE, MY YOUNGEST DAUGHTER, SIX YEARS OLD AT THE TIME, WAS VISITING ME. THINGS WEREN'T THE SAME. WE WERE WALKING DOWN THE STAIRS AND I HAD TO MAKE SURE SHE DIDN'T STEP ON A USED CONDOM. THERE WASN'T A DOOR ON OUR BATHROOM. THE HEATER MADE A CLANKING SOUND IN THE MIDDLE OF THE NIGHT. THE ART ON THE WALLS, WHICH ONCE LOOKED EXOTIC AND REAL TO ME, NOW LOOKED LIKE COLLAGES MADE BY KINDERGARTENERS.

NO SMOKING IN THE LOBBY

MOLLIE'S SHOCK OF RED HAIR LIT UP THE WHOLE BUILDING IN A WAY I NEVER SAW BEFORE.

BACK IN 1995 I HAD JUST FINISHED MY FIRST WEBSITE. I BUILT A WEBSITE FOR A RUSSIAN DIAMOND DEALER. THE RUSSIAN GAVE ME A BAG OF $17,500 IN CASH. IT'S THE FIRST TIME I EVER HAD MORE THAN $500 TO MY NAME.

I WENT STRAIGHT OVER TO THE CHELSEA HOTEL AND GOT MYSELF A ROOM FOR A YEAR, PAYING COMPLETELY IN ADVANCE. BACK IN THE 90'S PEOPLE DIDN'T KNOW WHAT TO DO WITH THEIR MONEY. THEY WERE GIVING IT AWAY.

EVERYTHING'S DIFFERENT NOW. I CAN'T TELL IF IT'S BECAUSE I'M OLDER OR IF MORE SHADES OF GRAY HAVE ENTERED INTO THE UNIVERSAL COLOR PALETTE.

WHEN I LAST MOVED INTO THE CHELSEA HOTEL (IN 2008) I WAS GOING THROUGH A MAJOR LIFE CHANGE AND NEEDED SOME PLACE I RECOGNIZED AS "HOME." WHEN I FINALLY LEFT THE HOTEL A FEW MONTHS LATER I HAD BEEN COMPLETELY REFRESHED. I HAD SPENT WEEKS AT A TIME TALKING TO NOBODY. I SCRIBBLED DOWN IDEAS AND THEN CROSSED THEM OUT AND QUICKLY FORGOT ABOUT THEM.

I HAD A FEVER ONCE FOR A FEW DAYS WHERE I THOUGHT MY BRAIN HAD BEEN TURNED INSIDE OUT AND LEFT TO DRY ON THE RADIATOR. SOMETIMES IT'S GOOD TO GO HOME TO GET A COMPLETELY FRESH START.

IN THOSE FEW MONTHS THE SLATE WIPED COMPLETELY CLEAN FOR ME. I HOPE I NEVER HAVE TO GO HOME AGAIN.

51

HOW TO BE A PSYCHIC IN 10 EASY LESSONS

I WAS IN A BAD STATE OF MIND BECAUSE I HAD RECENTLY SEPARATED FROM MY EX-WIFE. ANYTIME SOMEONE SEPARATES FROM SOMEONE THERE'S NEVER ANYTHING NICE ABOUT IT. MAYBE POLICE GET INVOLVED, MAYBE SOME NEIGHBORS, AND CERTAINLY THE CHILDREN. THE CHILDREN ARE ALWAYS INVOLVED.

2 DAYS EARLIER...

WHY DON'T YOU JOIN MY DAUGHTER AND I FOR THANKSGIVING?

BUT HER FIFTEEN-YEAR-OLD DAUGHTER PUT AN END TO THAT INVITATION.

MOM, I GOOGLED HIM AND HE'S *MARRIED!* WHY ARE YOU ALWAYS GOING OUT WITH MARRIED MEN??

AND, NOT HAVING ANYTHING ELSE TO DO, I WAS LYING ON THE FLOOR OF THE RANDOM HOTEL ROOM. SO I CAME UP WITH AN IDEA FOR SOMETHING TO DO: I WROTE AN AD AND PUT IT ON THE MOST AMAZING INTERNET INVENTION EVER:

CRAIGSLIST.

Feeling Psychic Today

Reply to: jaltucher@yahoogle.com

○ hide ◉ anonymize (will show as: xxxxxxxx@craigslist.org)

Posting Description:

I was very sick for a while. I would get piercing headaches all the time. But when the headaches finally stopped I realized I was psychic and could tell the future. I don't want this ability. But right now, today, I'm willing to answer any question that anyone emails me.

(Add / Edit Images)   (Continue)

52

I DON'T KNOW IF IT WAS SELFISH OR NOT. I WANTED TO HELP PEOPLE AND BY DOING SO, MAYBE THAT WOULD HELP MYSELF.

 "SHOULD I KEEP PURSUING THIS GUY AT WORK THAT I SLEPT WITH ONCE? WILL WE STILL BE TOGETHER A YEAR FROM NOW?"

"FIRST OFF, ANYTHING COULD HAPPEN. BUT AS LONG AS YOU'RE THINKING SO MUCH ABOUT THIS GUY, YOU'RE SPENDING ENERGY THAT COULD BE USED ON EITHER IMPROVING YOURSELF, OR DOING ACTIVITIES TO MEET OTHER GUYS. CHANCES ARE, YOU WON'T BE WITH THIS GUY IN A YEAR."

 "TELL ME SOMETHING ABOUT MYSELF THAT NOBODY KNOWS SO I KNOW YOU'RE A LEGITIMATE PSYCHIC."

"WHEN YOU WERE A LITTLE GIRL, YOU HAD LONG, BEAUTIFUL HAIR. BUT ONE DAY YOU GOT A HAIRCUT AND IT WAS CUT TOO SHORT. YOU CRIED ABOUT IT AND NO MATTER WHAT ANYONE TOLD YOU, YOU COULD NOT BE CONSOLED. YOU REMEMBER THAT TO THIS DAY."

"THAT'S *AMAZING!*"

 "I'M A DESIGNER OF CHILDREN'S CLOTHES. BUT I'M TIRED OF IT. I HAVE IDEAS ABOUT DOING NUTRITION CON-SULTING USING HOLISTIC METHODS COMBINING THE SPIRITUAL, THE PHYSICAL, ETC. WHAT SHOULD I DO?"

"START A BLOG WITH YOUR IDEAS. OFFER TO HAVE PEOPLE CONTACT YOU DIRECTLY FOR HELP. SUBMIT CONTENT TO MAGAZINES, OTHER BLOGS, ETC. COME UP WITH A 12-WEEK PLAN THAT PEOPLE CAN SIGN UP FOR WHERE THEY ACHIEVE GREATER HOLISTIC HEALTH BY THE END OF THE PLAN."

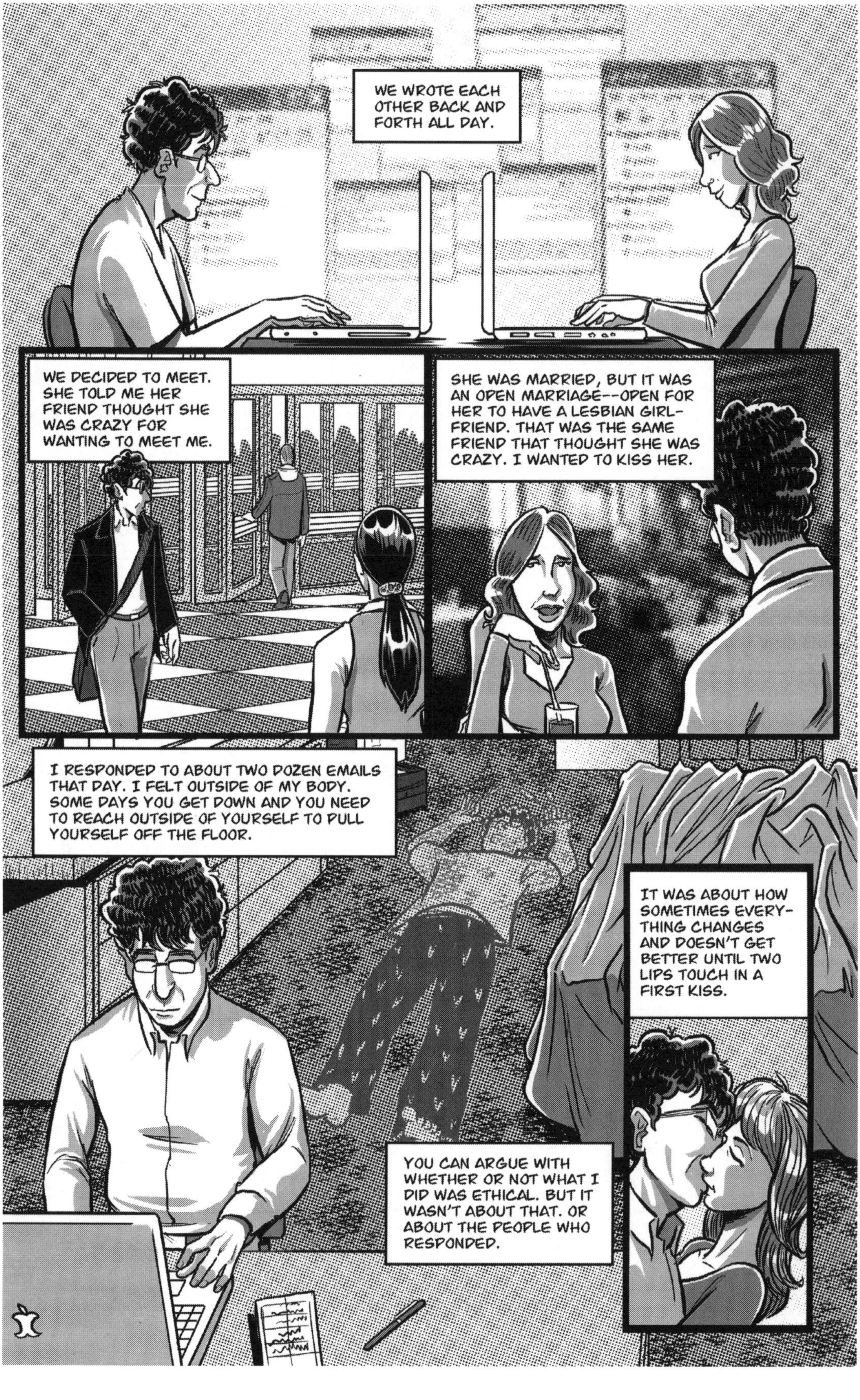
WE WROTE EACH OTHER BACK AND FORTH ALL DAY.
WE DECIDED TO MEET. SHE TOLD ME HER FRIEND THOUGHT SHE WAS CRAZY FOR WANTING TO MEET ME.
SHE WAS MARRIED, BUT IT WAS AN OPEN MARRIAGE--OPEN FOR HER TO HAVE A LESBIAN GIRL-FRIEND. THAT WAS THE SAME FRIEND THAT THOUGHT SHE WAS CRAZY. I WANTED TO KISS HER.
I RESPONDED TO ABOUT TWO DOZEN EMAILS THAT DAY. I FELT OUTSIDE OF MY BODY. SOME DAYS YOU GET DOWN AND YOU NEED TO REACH OUTSIDE OF YOURSELF TO PULL YOURSELF OFF THE FLOOR.
IT WAS ABOUT HOW SOMETIMES EVERY-THING CHANGES AND DOESN'T GET BETTER UNTIL TWO LIPS TOUCH IN A FIRST KISS.
YOU CAN ARGUE WITH WHETHER OR NOT WHAT I DID WAS ETHICAL. BUT IT WASN'T ABOUT THAT. OR ABOUT THE PEOPLE WHO RESPONDED.

I'M COMPLETELY HUMILIATED BY YOGA

I'M NOT FLEXIBLE, PLIABLE, AND MY BACK MUSCLES AREN'T RIPPED AND SHREDDED. I'VE NEVER STOOD ON MY HEAD. AND I GET EMBARRASSED WHEN I HEAR PEOPLE CHANT FOR RELIGIOUS REASONS.

SO, PRACTICING YOGA IN INDIA BECOMES A STORY OF HUMILIATION, WEAKNESS, DISAPPOINTMENT, AND FRUSTRATION FOR ME. AND I'M ONLY ON MY SECOND CLASS HERE. SOME OF THE THINGS THAT ARE HARD FOR ME SO FAR:

WORST IN CLASS. IN CLASS, I'M THE FIRST ONE WHO WAS FORCED TO STOP. I'M DRENCHED IN SWEAT. EVERYTHING HURTS. I SMELL LIKE THE GUTTER.

YOU STOP NOW.

EVERYONE LOOKS AT ME. I HAVE TO STAY UNTIL THE END OF THE CLASS BECAUSE WE ALL DO THE CLOSING MOVES TOGETHER. DO I LOOK BACK AT THEM? SHOULD I PRETEND I'M THE TEACHER AND THEY ARE ALL LOOKING BACK AT ME FOR APPROVAL? INSTEAD, I LOOK DOWN AND ACT LIKE I'M MEDITATING.

THE MEN IN THE CLASS ARE PERFECT. I SMELL LIKE SOMETHING IS DEAD IN THE WALLS OF YOUR HOUSE. THE OTHER GUYS TAKE THEIR SHIRTS OFF. THEY HAVE MUSCLES IN PLACES CALLED TIBIAS, FEMURS, PSOAS. PARTS OF THE BODY I NEVER HEARD OF. LIKE WHEN YOU SUDDENLY LOOK AT A MAP OF THE WORLD AND REALIZE FOR THE FIRST TIME THAT AFRICA IS BROKEN UP INTO MANY TINY COUNTRIES THAT YOU NEVER KNEW EXISTED AND MOST LIKELY WILL NEVER VISIT.

MY SECRET REVEALED. I WAS JUST PRETENDING TO BE HERE.

RELAX YOUR ARM, STRETCH IT OUT THIS WAY.

LEG WANTS TO GO HERE!

JUST LET THE FINGERS FROM MY LEFT HAND CLASP THE FINGERS FROM MY RIGHT HAND SO THEY LEAVE.

YOGA VISION. YOGA SUPPOSEDLY MAKES YOUR EYES SHINE BRIGHTER. THIS IS WHAT CLAUDIA TELLS ME. ALL OF THE ADVANCED STUDENTS LOOK AT ME WITH THEIR HEAT VISION. I MELTED INTO THE DUST.

SANSKRIT. AT BREAKFAST AT A LOCAL RESTAURANT THERE WERE NO INDIANS. ONLY YOGA STUDENTS.

I HAD TROUBLE WITH UTTHITA HASTA PADANGUSTHASANA.

I FINALLY GOT PAST ARDHA BADDHA PADMA PASCHIMOTTANASANA.

CHANTING. AT THE BEGINNING OF CLASS THERE'S A CHANT. I CAN HANDLE THAT. BUT THEN IT GOES INTO SOMETHING ELSE THAT I CAN'T UNDERSTAND. EVERYONE ELSE IS DOING THE CHANT. FOR SOME REASON I BLUSH AND I TRY TO HUM ALONG WITH IT BUT THEN BLUSH MORE BECAUSE WHY AM I EVEN HUMMING?

OOOHHMMM OOOOHHHMMMM OOOHHMMM

HMMHMM ♪

EARNESTNESS.

IT'S GOOD IT'S CROWDED. MORE PEOPLE ARE DOING YOGA.

I'M NOT SURE HOW TO RESPOND. MAYBE, "I FEEL LIKE WORLD PEACE MIGHT BE RIGHT AROUND THE CORNER." OR, "IF ONLY EVERYONE HAD A FULLY DEVELOPED TIBIA MUSCLE, LESS PEOPLE MIGHT GET DIVORCED."

COCONUTS. AFTER PRACTICE ON THE FIRST DAY I WAS SWEATING SO MUCH I THOUGHT I WOULD HAVE NO MORE WATER LEFT IN MY BODY.

DRINK COCONUT JUICE. IT WILL GIVE YOU ELECTROLYTES.

WE'RE MONKEYS FROM A MILLION GENERATIONS AGO AND WE NEED OUR COCONUTS SO WE CAN MATE AND HAVE CHILDREN. BUT I DON'T LIKE COCONUT JUICE.

COLD SHOWER. I'M NOT QUITE USED TO THE SMELL OF THE WATER HERE YET. I AM SAYING THIS VERY POLITELY. AND I COULDN'T FIGURE OUT HOW TO GET HOT WATER. SO I TOOK A FREEZING COLD SHOWER AND COULDN'T GET THE SOAP OFF MY SKIN.

IT'S DAY FOUR AND I'M LOVING EVERY MINUTE OF MY TRIP HERE. TOMORROW IS MY THIRD CLASS.

THE EASIEST WAY TO SUCCEED AS AN ENTREPRENEUR

I WAS THE WORST PIZZA DELIVERY GUY.

I ALSO NEVER GOT TIPS.

WENDE, MY PARTNER IN OUR RESTAURANT DELIVERY BUSINESS, ALWAYS GOT TIPS. AND I SECRETLY LOVED HER. I COULDN'T COMPETE. I ALWAYS HOPED I WOULD DELIVER TO A FRAT PARTY WHERE ALL THE GIRLS WERE RUNNING AROUND NAKED. BUT THAT NEVER HAPPENED.

WE ALSO STARTED A DEBIT CARD FOR COLLEGE KIDS. FROM THE FIRST DAY WE WERE OPEN FOR BUSINESS WE HAD COLLEGE KIDS SIGNING UP FOR OUR CARD (THERE WERE NO CREDIT CARDS FOR KIDS THEN). AND ANYONE WHO HAD OUR DEBIT CARD COULD ORDER FOOD FROM THE 20 OR SO RESTAURANTS IN TOWN AND WE'D DELIVER, BUT WITH A 25% MARKUP.

I LOVED DELIVERING FOOD BECAUSE IT GAVE ME TWENTY, OR EVEN FORTY-MINUTE BREAKS FROM MY GIRLFRIEND. I WAS A SCREWED UP 19-YEAR-OLD THEN.

NOW I'M ONLY A MILDLY-SCREWED-UP 43-YEAR-OLD. I'VE HAD SEVEN STARTUPS SINCE THEN. AND SOME PROFITABLE EXITS. AND ANOTHER 20 OR SO THAT I'VE FUNDED.

WHEN I THINK "ENTREPRENEUR," I THINK MARK CUBAN OR LARRY PAGE OR STEVE JOBS. I DON'T USUALLY THINK OF MYSELF. IN PART BECAUSE I FEEL SHAME THAT AFTER ALL OF THESE STARTUPS I DON'T HAVE A BILLION DOLLARS. MANY STARTUPS FAIL. BUT I'VE HAD A FEW SUCCESSES AS WELL.

SUCCESS IN A STARTUP MAKES YOU FEEL IMMORTAL.

I WAS GOING TO MAKE THIS "THE 12 RULES TO BEING A GOOD ENTREPRENEUR" AND I OUTLINED THE 12 RULES THAT HAVE CONSISTENTLY WORKED FOR ME. BUT RULE #1 IS TAKING UP 1500 WORDS ALREADY. SO THIS ONE RULE IS GOING TO TAKE UP THE WHOLE STORY. BUT, FOR ME, THIS IS THE MOST IMPORTANT RULE.

THE MOST IMPORTANT RULE: HAVE A CUSTOMER BEFORE YOU START YOUR BUSINESS.

IF YOU HAVE TO WORK FOR TWO YEARS BEFORE ONE DOLLAR OF REVENUE COMES INTO YOUR BUSINESS THEN THAT'S TOO MUCH WORK. I'M LAZY SO I LIKE MONEY COMING IN WITH AS LITTLE WORK AS POSSIBLE.

MARK ZUCKERBERG, OF COURSE, IS DIFFERENT. HE PUT IN YEARS OF WORK BEFORE DOLLAR ONE OF REVENUE CAME IN. BUT WE'RE DIFFERENT PEOPLE.

FAKE RULE: EXECUTION IS IMPORTANT.

EXECUTION IS USELESS. THE ONLY THING THAT'S IMPORTANT IS MONEY. YOU GET MONEY BY HAVING A CUSTOMER. YOU GET A CUSTOMER BY SATISFYING A NEED THAT'S SO IMPORTANT TO THEM THEY WOULD BE WILLING TO PAY FOR IT. IF YOU HAVE A CUSTOMER THAT'S WILLING TO PAY YOU MONEY, THEN EXECUTION BECOMES A LOT EASIER. LIFE AS AN ENTREPRENEUR IS HARD. WHY MAKE IT HARDER?

FOR EXAMPLE, THIS IS HOW STOCKPICKR STARTED...

MID 2006.

TOM CLARKE

HEY JAMES, LET'S GET TOGETHER OVER LUNCH AND BRAINSTORM. HOW'S YOUR SCHEDULE IN TWO WEEKS?

I CALLED UP A DEVELOPMENT FIRM IN INDIA. MYSPACE HAD JUST BEEN ACQUIRED BY NEWSCORP SO I SKETCHED OUT WHAT I CONSIDERED THE "MYSPACE OF FINANCE." IN OTHER WORDS, I WANTED TO CREATE A SITE THAT I WOULD USE AS A PROFESSIONAL TRADER SO I KNEW OTHER TRADERS WOULD BENEFIT FROM IT. AND, I HAD A THEORY ABOUT MAKING A QUALITY FINANCIAL SITE THAT BASICALLY HAD NO NEWS IN IT. I'M GOING TO BE BLUNT: 99% OF FINANCIAL NEWS IS USELESS AND MISINFORMED AND MISLEADING, IF NOT OUTRIGHT LYING.

WITHIN A WEEK, FOR FREE (BECAUSE I TOLD THE COMPANY IN INDIA THAT I WOULD BE BUILDING THE SITE WITH THEM IF THEY SENT BACK GOOD SCREENSHOTS, WHICH WAS TRUE), THE COMPANY SENT ME BACK SCREENSHOTS.

I'M ALMOST DONE WITH THE SITE. HERE IT IS. I'M ALSO TALKING WITH YAHOO AND AOL AS WELL. *

WHY ARE YOU TALKING WITH THEM? YOU'VE BEEN WITH US FOREVER. LET'S DO THIS TOGETHER.

GREAT. HOW ABOUT YOU GUYS TAKE 10% OF THE COMPANY AND PUT ALL YOUR EXTRA ADS ON ALL OF OUR PAGES AND LET ME LINK FROM EVERY ARTICLE BACK TO STOCKPICKR.COM.

I THOUGHT WE WERE PARTNERS. LET'S DO IT 50-50.

*I HAD SET UP MEETINGS WITH YAHOO AND AOL SO IT WASN'T A STRETCH TO SAY. NOBODY WANTS TO BE THE FIRST CUSTOMER, SO YOU HAVE TO CREATE THE AURA OF MANY CUSTOMERS.

SO RIGHT AWAY, I HAD GIVEN UP 50% OF THE COMPANY. MOST PEOPLE I SPOKE TO THOUGHT THIS WAS A HORRIBLE IDEA. BUT GIVING 50% OF YOUR COMPANY AWAY IS OFTEN BETTER THAN GIVING 10% OF YOUR COMPANY AWAY. WHEN YOU GIVE 50% OF THE COMPANY AWAY, YOUR PARTNER IS OBLIGATED TO FOLLOW THROUGH AND BE A REAL PARTNER. HE CAN NEVER FORGET ABOUT YOU. AGAIN, IT'S ALL ABOUT MAKING LIFE EASY. WITH FAMILY RESPONSIBILITIES, HEALTH, LIFE IN GENERAL, WHY MAKE THINGS EVEN HARDER?

1. I WAS GOING TO GET TRAFFIC

SO, AT THAT POINT, WITHOUT EVEN HAVING A SITE FINISHED (OR EVEN STARTED) I KNEW I HAD THREE THINGS GOING FOR ME: THESTREET.COM GOT 100MM PAGEVIEWS A MONTH SO I KNEW I WOULD GET SOME PERCENTAGE OF THAT.

2. I WAS GOING TO MAKE MONEY

IF I GOT EVEN 3 MILLION PAGEVIEWS A MONTH AND THE AVERAGE CPM OF THESTREET.COM WAS $17, I WOULD MAKE ABOUT $50,000 A MONTH WITH EXPENSES NEARING ZERO.

3. PROFITABILITY FROM DAY ONE!

PROFITABILITY AND GROWTH FROM DAY ONE MEANT I COULD PUT THE COMPANY UP FOR SALE ALMOST IMMEDIATELY. BUT THAT'S ANOTHER STORY.

WITH MY FIRST SUCCESSFUL COMPANY, RESET, I HAD ABOUT 10 PAYING CUSTOMERS BEFORE I FINALLY MADE THE JUMP TO RUNNING THE COMPANY FULLTIME: HBO, INTERSCOPE, BMG, NEW LINE CINEMA, AND WARNER BROTHERS WERE ALL PAYING CUSTOMERS BEFORE I JUMPED SHIP FROM HBO TO RUN RESET FULLTIME.

WHEN I STARTED MY FUND OF HEDGE FUNDS I DIDN'T PUT ONE DIME INTO THE EXPENSE OF SETTING IT UP UNTIL I HAD THE FIRST $20 MILLION COMMITMENT. IT TOOK A YEAR OF CULTIVATING MY NETWORK BEFORE I HAD THAT COMMITMENT, BUT IT WORKED.

THIS IS JUST ME, PERSONALLY. SOME PEOPLE DON'T MIND STARTING A COMPANY WITHOUT ANY CUSTOMERS. I'M TOO CONSERVATIVE FOR THIS. I'M HAPPY TO EVEN GIVE UP EQUITY TO GET THAT FIRST CUSTOMER. 50% OF A PROFITABLE COMPANY IS BETTER THAN 100% OF A COMPANY THAT WILL PROBABLY QUICKLY GO OUT OF BUSINESS.

HOW DO YOU GET THAT FIRST CUSTOMER?

WHO LIST THE 20 CEO'S OR HIGH LEVEL EXECUTIVES YOU WOULD LIKE TO MEET. IF YOU HAVE A ROLODEX, GREAT. IF YOU DON'T, THEN YOU MIGHT HAVE TO WRITE TO 40 PEOPLE. BUT IT'S OK IF YOUR ROLODEX IS COLD. MANY SUCCESSFUL BUSINESSES I'VE BEEN INVOLVED WITH STARTED WITH COLD EMAILS.

IDEA DEVELOP 20 IDEAS FOR EACH PERSON.

COMMUNICATE WRITE THEM ALL, GIVING AT LEAST 10 OF THE IDEAS, IN DETAIL, AND HOW YOU WOULD IMPLEMENT THEM.

MEET ALL THIS DOES IS GET YOU THE MEETING. ONCE YOU'RE IN THE DOOR, THE CONVERSATION CAN GO ANYWHERE. OF THE 20 PEOPLE YOU WRITE, RULE OF THE UNIVERSE IS YOU'LL GET SIX MEETINGS.

ASK IN THE MEETINGS ASK THE QUESTION, *"WHAT ONE PRODUCT CAN I BUILD FOR YOU THAT YOU WILL DEFINITELY BUY?"* BECAUSE OF GLOBALIZATION YOU CAN BUILD ANYTHING FOR CHEAP. I BUILT THE FIRST WORKING VERSION OF STOCKPICKR.COM FOR $3000 IN BANGALORE. THROW IN ANOTHER $150 FROM A DESIGN MADE IN SIBERIA. YOU NEED ZERO SKILL SET FOR THAT. JUST A GOOD IDEA MUSCLE, AN ABILITY TO SELL, AND MODEST ABILITY TO MANAGE A PROJECT.

NEVER SAY NO NEVER. IF SOMEONE SAYS, "CAN YOU DO THIS?" YES. "BUT CAN YOU DO THIS?" YES. "CAN YOU DO IT FOR THIS?" YES. FOLLOW UP EVERY DAY. NICE TO MEET YOU. HERE'S MY SKETCH OF WHAT YOU WANT. SHOULD I START TODAY?

EQUITY IF NECESSARY, GIVE UP EQUITY FOR THAT FIRST CUSTOMER. OR FIRST TWO CUSTOMERS.

DONE IF MORE THAN ONE CEO WANTS THE SAME PRODUCT OR SERVICE, AND THE PRICE IS RIGHT, THEN NOW YOU HAVE A BUSINESS. BUILD THE PRODUCT, SELL IT, AND YOU'RE IN SHAPE.

REPEAT YOU'RE NOT REALLY "DONE." EVERY DAY YOU HAVE TO GO BACK AND SEE IF YOUR CUSTOMER IS ACHIEVING MORE SUCCESS BECAUSE OF YOUR PRODUCTS. IF HE IS, THEN ASK HIM WHAT ELSE HE NEEDS AND THEN BUILD IT. IF HE ISN'T, THEN ASK HIM WHAT ELSE HE NEEDS AND BUILD IT. YOUR EASIEST NEW SALES WILL BE WITH YOUR OLD CUSTOMERS.

THIS HAS WORKED FOR ME ON THREE DIFFERENT OCCASIONS. AND EACH TIME RESULTED IN GREAT PROFITS FOR ME.*

*THIS TECHNIQUE HAS ALSO WORKED FOR PEOPLE WHO HAVE CONTACTED ME WITH THEIR OWN IDEAS.

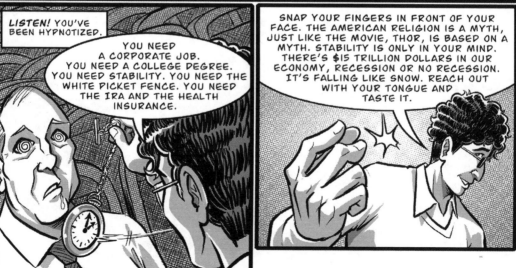

LISTEN! YOU'VE BEEN HYPNOTIZED.

YOU NEED A CORPORATE JOB. YOU NEED A COLLEGE DEGREE. YOU NEED STABILITY. YOU NEED THE WHITE PICKET FENCE. YOU NEED THE IRA AND THE HEALTH INSURANCE.

SNAP YOUR FINGERS IN FRONT OF YOUR FACE. THE AMERICAN RELIGION IS A MYTH, JUST LIKE THE MOVIE, THOR, IS BASED ON A MYTH. STABILITY IS ONLY IN YOUR MIND. THERE'S $15 TRILLION DOLLARS IN OUR ECONOMY, RECESSION OR NO RECESSION. IT'S FALLING LIKE SNOW. REACH OUT WITH YOUR TONGUE AND TASTE IT.

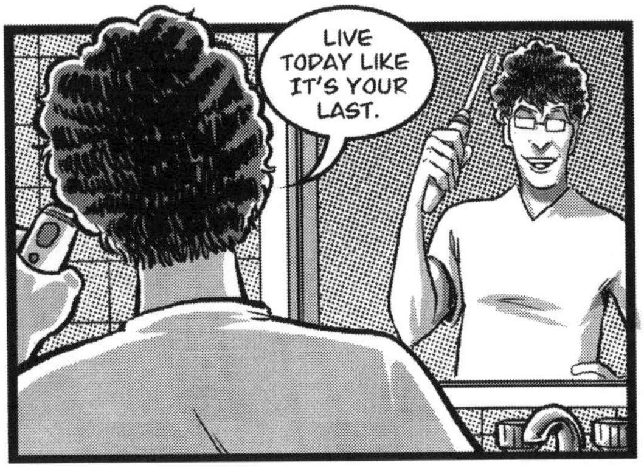
LIVE TODAY LIKE IT'S YOUR LAST.

About the Author

James Altucher has sold 4 businesses and written 7 books. He's lost everything again and again but keeps coming back. He's written about failure, loss, success, women, and how it feels to pull yourself off the floor in your lowest moments and force yourself to DO IT again. And again. He's written for the *Wall Street Journal, The Financial Times,* and a dozen other newspapers and prominent websites. He regularly appears on TV spouting nonsense about many things. He's uglier than the way he's drawn in this comic book. His last book was *I Was Blind But Now I See.* He blogs at jamesaltucher.com and lives on twitter at @jaltucher.

Nathan Lueth

came into existence with a pencil in his hand, a feat that continues to confound obstetricians to this day. No one knows for sure when he started drawing or where his love of comics came from, but most experts agree that his professional career began after graduating from the Minneapolis College of Art and Design, as a caricaturist in the Mall of America. Soon he was freelance illustrating for the likes of Target, General Mills, and Stone Arch Books.

When not drawing comics for other people, Nathan draws his own super awesome fantasy webcomic, *Impure Blood* (www.impurebloodwebcomic.com). He is proud to be a part of Writers of the Round Table, as he believes that comics should be for everyone, not just nerds (it should be noted that he may be trying to turn the general population into nerds). With Round Table he has illustrated *Overachievement* by Dr. John Eliot (April 2011) and a colored adaptation of *The U.S. Constitution* (March 2012). He resides in St. Paul, Minnesota, with a cat, a turtle, and his imminent wife, Nadja, upon whom he performs his nerd conversion experiments.

Nadja Baer has been a words-nerd all her life. She speaks English, German, Italian, and Spanish (with varying degrees of fluency), can teach Taekwondo classes in Korean, and is currently working on expanding her French vocabulary. Since receiving a Bachelor's degree in Creative Writing at the University of Minnesota, she has served as the office thesaurus, dictionary, translator, and spell-checker in every one of her day jobs. She wrote her first terrible novella at the age of eight, and is now focused on writing comics and novels for young adults. Her work can be seen for free in the online graphic novel, *Impure Blood* (www.impurebloodwebcomic.com), which is drawn by her soon-to-be husband. Other projects she has scripted for Round Table include *Everything's Okay* (Sept 2011), *Delivering Happiness* (March 2012), and an adaptation of *The U.S. Constitution* (March 2012). Aside from a love of a good story with pretty pictures, they share a house, a cat, a turtle, and a belief that more people should embrace their inner nerd.

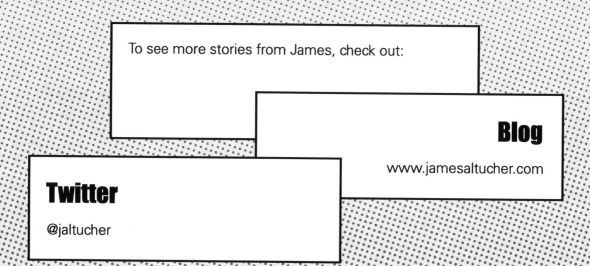

To see more stories from James, check out:

Blog

www.jamesaltucher.com

Twitter

@jaltucher

James' Latest Book: *I Was Blind But Now I See*,
available on Amazon in paperback and Kindle.

JAMES

I WAS BLIND BUT NOW I SEE

ALTUCHER

MY JOURNEY SURVIVING CHILDHOOD CANCER

Everything's Okay

A ROUND TABLE COMIC

ALESIA
SHUTE

ILLUSTRATED BY
NATHAN
LUETH

rtc
ROUND TABLE
COMICS

AVAILABLE NOW FROM
ROUND TABLE COMICS

Based on the book *From the Barrio to the Board Room*

I HAVE BEEN KNIFED...

...SHOT AT...

AND BEAT UP MORE TIMES THAN I CARE TO DISCUSS, AND I GAVE BACK MORE THAN MY FAIR SHARE AS WELL.

IT DOESN'T MATTER IF YOU'RE CAREFUL OR NOT, IT ALL EVENTUALLY CATCHES UP WITH YOU. YOU MIGHT NOT GET CAUGHT, BUT YOU WILL STILL HAVE TO LIVE WITH WHAT YOU HAVE DONE, AND GUILT IS A HEAVY BURDEN.

HAVING LIVED THROUGH THE VIOLENCE ON THE STREET, I CAN TELL YOU THAT GANGBANGING IS NOT A LIFESTYLE, IT'S A 'DEATH-STYLE.'

Mi Barrio

"DON'T LET WHERE YOU CAME FROM DICTATE WHO YOU ARE, BUT LET IT BE PART OF WHO YOU BECOME."

ROBERT RENTERIA
As told to Corey Michael Blake
Shane Clester

AVAILABLE WHERE BOOKS ARE SOLD
WWW.FROMTHEBARRIO.COM

MACHIAVELLI

ADAPTED &
ILLUSTRATED BY

SHANE
CLESTER

The Prince

A ROUND TABLE COMICS

"The politics of Europe render it indispensably
necessary that we be one nation only,
firmly held together."

-Thomas Jefferson

THE UNITED STATES CONSTITUTION

A Graphic Novel

COMING SPRING 2012

rtc
ROUND TABLE
COMICS

rtc
ROUND TABLE
COMICS

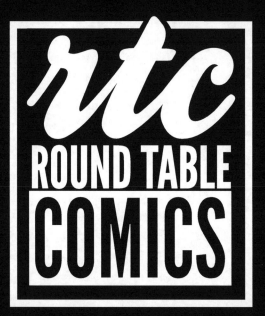

@RndTableComics